From Horses to Cyberspace

David and Helga Compston

From Horses to Cyberspace

Olympia Publishers
London

www.olympiapublishers.com
OLYMPIA PAPERBACK EDITION

A CIP catalogue record for this title is
available from the British Library.

ISBN: 978-1-84897-852-2

First Published in 2019

Olympia Publishers
60 Cannon Street
London
EC4N 6NP

Printed in Great Britain

For George and Hugo

Acknowledgements

To write a biography is to write a memoir and in so doing we realise that our lives and experiences owe everything to the people with whom we have shared them. We owe so many a thank you for their contributions and have endeavoured to bring many of them into the story.

Our thanks to Graham Meare, our brother- in- law, without his IT skills we would have never reached the stage when we could approach our publisher. David's sister's encouragement and Judith's knowledge of the family histories have given a depth to the story and our thanks go to her for that important contribution and her tolerance during the many hours Graham worked at his computer for us. Also thanks to our grandsons George and Hugo for their IT support

Michael Alexander's photographic skill is beautifully demonstrated in the photograph of Howtown Ullswater and we thank him for the time and trouble he took to produce this image and for his permission to use it. We also thank him for his valuable input in how to arrange the images to support the text.

Sue Horsler's contribution in preparing the typeset proof with the images in place embedded in the text represented a major step forward towards publication and we thank her for that important input to the work. Also we thank her for the invaluable work she did in revising the text and images arrangement following the proofreading

Without the Stockton Family Society our links to Helga's American 'cousins' would never have been known to us. We add our acknowledgement to Susie Stockton-Link for her many years of service as secretary of the society.

Our thanks to Constance M. Greif and Wanda S. Gunning whose book *MORVEN, MEMORY, MYTH & REALITY* has provided us with the background of the American Stocktons' contribution to American history.

Stephen Maynard provided the information on the history of the Maynard/ Meyer-Udewald family for which we thank him.

We thank our friends Elizabeth Raine and Jim Kent for proofreading the first draft.

John Sullivan's photograph of us on the cover is very flattering somehow making us look much younger than we are. And he did not 'airbrush' it! So we thank John for his photographic skills and for permission to use the picture.

We acknowledge the write-up on the Internet by those at Ferrybridge on the day when the cooling towers collapsed and the quick response of the station chemist who took the dramatic photographs of the tower collapsing.

A special thanks to poets Mike & Lesley Liston and Reg & Monica Jeune for *THE ALLOTT & LOMAX LUNCHEON – AN APPRECIATION*.

We thank John Roberts, David's business partner, for checking the accuracy of the history of Allotts and adding to the story relating to theme park rides and the London Eye.

Also our thanks to George Carpenter who confirmed our recollections of the return of Bobby Moore to Mexico from Bogota for the 1970 World Cup.

Our thanks to the author Joanne Lake who kindly gave us the most valuable guidance in relation to arranging publication.

ALAMY gave vital support providing many of the images for which we thank them.

We thank our publishers for scrutinizing the manuscript, their constructive critism and amending wording where appropriate.

Contents

INTRODUCTION
by
David Compston

Helga and I were born before the Second World War. Helga was three when the War started, I was only one. She can recollect her life from those early War years. She was sent away from her parents in Sale near Manchester to live with the farmer friends of her aunt Nora on the north Yorkshire coast at Staintondale, halfway between Scarborough and Whitby. So, she was in a sense an evacuee, but unlike most evacuees who were sent to families they did not know, she lived with friends of her family. I was born at Rosthwaite in Borrowdale Cumberland and my first recollections are of living with my mother in the remote hamlet of Howtown on the shores of Ullswater. My father was away in the army and my life at that time was that of a child in a single-parent family.

As the prospects for a successful outcome to the War improved, Helga returned to her parents and her younger sister in suburban Sale. I continued to live round Ullswater with my mother until soon after the War ended and my father was demobbed. We then moved to Mellor, an outer suburb to the south of Manchester.

Neither of us took to life in suburbia after our formative years of remote country life.

My schooling was mostly as a boarder, in Lincolnshire and then in North London. Helga went to the local schools and then to private college near her home in Sale.

We each have a sister, Helga's being two years younger than her and mine being six and a half years younger than me. Both had quite different early formative years to us, being brought up with both parents at home in the Cheshire suburbs of Manchester.

Towards the end of my schooling, my parents were in the early stages of their marriage breaking up and my public schooling was curtailed after one term in the lower sixth form. Inspired by reading the lives and achievements of the great engineers of the Industrial Revolution and the Victorian Era, I chose a career as a civil engineer and left school to be an articled trainee engineer at the Manchester Ship Canal Company. During this period of five years of practical training, I attended evening classes with some day release classes to obtain the equivalent qualifications of a graduate of engineering from a university.

Helga started work at sixteen as a secretary near Manchester.

My sport was rugby, Helga's was tennis. She was also a dancing girl in the local amateur dramatic society. The rugby men and the tennis and dancing girls shared the same social life in Sale, which in the main was confined to Friday and Saturday evenings at the sports club dances. This brought us together.

After our marriage, we lived in south Yorkshire. I had completed my engineering courses and joined the consulting engineers, C. S. Allott & Son. After a short period in the design office in Sale, I had been transferred to the staff supervising the construction of Ferrybridge 'C' Power Station, one of the world's largest, and consequently became involved in one of the most major engineering failures of the twentieth century. Helga gave up work to run our first home which we rented in the small village of Birkin in the country between Ferrybridge and Selby.

After my time on site at Ferrybridge, I was transferred back to our head office in Sale. Although this remained my office for the rest of my professional career, it was in fact a base from which I travelled the world as a consulting engineer.

When we returned to Cheshire, Helga and I were determined to find a home in the country. We had no money. However, we knew how country society worked, with who you knew being important. So, we found a cottage in the country to rent.

Our only child James was born just after we moved into our newly found home. Helga continued her role as a housewife and now a mother, the normal role of a young middle-class married woman at that time.

For the rest of my professional career, I worked on major projects as far apart as Latin America and Hong Kong, becoming a director and then chairman of the group of Allott companies.

Helga consequently had a very full life looking after James, myself and later on, the older family members, being as she puts it, a professional housewife, overseeing James's upbringing, driving him to and from boarding school in Lincolnshire and then North London, while also looking after our homes and gardens.

While we enjoyed life in our Cheshire cottage, we still wanted part of our life in a country area more remote from a city. We found a retreat on the Lowther Estate near Penrith in what was by then Cumbria. Here, throughout James's childhood we had holidays and weekends.

Helga became very involved in charity work and in support of the Conservative Party as well as playing a key role in the company's corporate entertainment both in the UK and round the world.

During the time I was chairman of Allotts, the company secured the important contract for overseeing the design, fabrication and erection of the London Eye. I also became involved in economic development and the government training programmes in Manchester, when I was fortunate to play a part in the renaissance of the city.

Although in my youth I was a keen rugby player, it was while I was involved in training and economic development at the end of my career that I had my most exciting involvement in sport as a member of the organising committee of the 2002 Manchester Commonwealth Games.

As I write this in my retirement, I know I could not have had such an interesting career without the full support and encouragement of Helga and I can admire the home Helga has created for us during our marriage with her collection of antiques and china, together with our art collection.

We have researched our family histories back to the late 1400s and in doing so have established that Helga has a common ancestor with Richard Stockton, one of the signers of the American Declaration of Independence.

So, this is the story of our family, our home and business lives from the time of being two children living in the War years, through the great changes from the austerity of those War years and the time when horses were still a source of power on farms, to the era dominated by information technology and instant communication for all, most of which is being transmitted through cyberspace.

Now it seems the right to privacy is lost with an ever-increasing data base which contains ones most confidential information accessible to a vast number of people across the world, where free speech that we all treasured in the United Kingdom no longer exists, being compromised by laws passed relating to racial discrimination and discussion on religion may cause offence leading to court action. We are now not at liberty to decide on every day risks to be taken lest we fall foul of health and safety laws which are destroying an important element of freedom to make personal judgments of how life can be conducted. British culture, which had been firmly based on Christian principles, is now changing to a multicultural society with an ever-increasing proportion of the population introducing very different lifestyles and religious beliefs.

I decided that this story should be told because I believe those reading it will find this record of our life from the earlier part of the twentieth century into the twenty-first century, with its dramatic changes in lifestyle and attitude to life during that period, fascinating.

1. Harvesting pre-World War II

CHAPTER ONE
The Formative Years

Helga was born in Sale Cottage Hospital near Manchester on 16th March 1936. Her father, Richard (Dick) Lee Postlethwaite, was from a Carlisle family and worked in the distribution of Harvo, a well-known brand of malt bread. Her mother, Marjorie, who worked in sales in the cotton trade, was from the Stockton family of Cheshire although her parents had lived in Monton north-west of Manchester. All Helga's grandparents had died before Helga was born. Her sister Alison was born in March 1938.

David was born in the front bedroom of his grandparents' home, Hazel Bank, an imposing house on the hillside overlooking the village of Rosthwaite in Borrowdale in Cumberland on 21st October 1938. His father, Denis, was an accountant with the Manchester Corporation Electricity Department, having been brought up in Kensington in London. David's mother, Nancy Doreen, had been brought up from being a very young girl in Rosthwaite, where her parents, William and Clara Badrock, who were hoteliers, had moved their business from Yorkshire. In Yorkshire, they were running three hotels, in Ripon, York and the Racehorses at Grassington in Wharfedale. Seeing the potential of the Lake District as a future major tourist area, they took over the Scafell Hotel in Borrowdale just after the First World War. They did not own the actual property which was bought many years later by their son Samuel (Sandy).

2. Hazel Bank

The declaration of war on Germany on 3rd September 1939 had a profound impact on the earliest years of Helga's childhood.

War Declared
September 1939

3.

4.

At some time in the early part of the War, her parents sent her to live with the Cross family who had the largest farm in Staintondale on the north Yorkshire coast about halfway between Scarborough and Whitby. Helga's aunt Nora lived in Staintondale and her and the Cross family were friends. At that time children were being evacuated from the major cities to live with families in the countryside, most not even knowing which family they would be joining when they said goodbye to their parents on their city railway stations with a label tied round their necks to say who they were.

5. Evacuee Children World War II

While Helga might therefore be described as having been an evacuee, she was going to live with friends of her family unlike most evacuees. Her baby sister remained with her mother and father in Sale. Helga does not know exactly when she was sent away to

Yorkshire, but it would have been after the War was declared in late 1939 or early 1940. She was certainly old enough to be aware at that time she had a baby sister. But she was not old enough to be expected to recall in her later life the event of her departure to join a new family a long way away from her parents and baby sister. Nor was she ever told exactly what motivated her parents to make that decision. She believed that her parents, expecting that Manchester would suffer severe bombing, wished her to be away from that danger.

There is no doubt that the separation from her parents had a psychological impact on her. She has absolutely no doubt that she was very happy as the youngest child in the Cross household, the youngest of Mr and Mrs Cross's five children was Gladys, being about fourteen years older than little Helga. Helga looked on Mrs Cross as her own mother.

So, Helga became unaware of the family she had left behind in Sale. She does not know exactly how long she lived with the Cross family. She remembers the life on the two hundred-acre farm where two heavy horses provided the power in the fields and she looked for and collected eggs from the barn and churned the butter. She recalls routines such as the weekly wash, bread being made in the kitchen coal fire range oven and Sundays, when after chapel and lunch, the family sat and read appropriate material for Methodists. Although she was very young, she must have learnt to read as her reading material was the *ENCYCLOPEDIA BRITANNICA*! She was also allowed to read the magazine called *THE GIRLS' FRIEND*. On Sunday evenings, there would be music with Mrs Cross playing the piano and her sons, George and Arthur, playing the violin and the cello. Helga sang.

However, she only remembers two specific incidents during

this period. She was being bathed when a German bomber fleeing for home dropped its load near the house. She remembers vividly the explosion and the impact of the blast which nearly blew in the glass of the window and then nearly sucked it out. She says she can see the effect on that glass to this day as the water in the bath surged up and nearly spilt over the floor with the whole house shaking. She also remembers falling into a snowdrift while walking back to the farm with her little friend from Sunday school and the sound of the wind in the telephone wires. That sound she has loved, as well as the sound of a storm wind, all her life. Those two incidents are her first specific memories of incidents in her life.

Her next memory is of being told by Mrs Cross that the little girl walking down the lane to the farm was her sister. "I did not know I had a little sister," Helga said. Her parents had come to take her home to Sale.

6. Helga at Cross's Farm *7. "Sister I didn't know I had."* *8. Helga – First Colour Photograph*

She was four in March 1940. Helga does not remember going to school in Staintondale. It would therefore probably in 1941, when Helga would have been due to start the school year after her fifth birthday, when she returned to Sale. While horse power was still the main source of power in farming, British technology had developed sophisticated radar with a chain of radar stations covering south-east England, while the Germans up to this time had not placed priority on radar development. British engineering had produced the Spitfire and

9. Prime Minister, Churchill

Hurricane which the German fighters could not match. By the spring of 1940 British academics had cracked the German secret code to give the RAF information on Luftwaffe movements. All this resulted in Germany losing the Battle of Britain. The main bombing of Manchester had taken place in late 1940 and now the danger was much diminished.

She started school at Worthington Road Primary School in Sale Moor where she was tied to a drainpipe and teased because of her Yorkshire accent.

Even today, she finds it difficult to believe she was probably nearly into her sixth year before she rejoined her own family. She never bonded with her mother although she loved her father. Clearly, her experience of living away from her parents and her sister in her earliest formative years was a happy period in her life. However, the impact of then finding she had parents and a sister caused some profound impact on her to the extent that her memories of individual events in her life up to that time have been lost, except for two specific incidents. She thinks that she was too young to have such memories. Perhaps she is right, but perhaps they were blocked out by the shock of such a sudden change in her life on leaving a happy country home in Yorkshire to live in the unfamiliar surroundings of suburbia.

10. Eight-Year-Old Helga Still Part of the Cross Family

David was just over ten months old when the War broke out. His father, Denis, was in the Territorial Army (TA - part time army reserve) and was at the TA annual camp as the crisis leading up to the War was intensifying. Whilst there, he received a letter from His Majesty King George VI stating that it was his pleasure to invite Denis to join the regular army, an invitation that clearly Denis felt could not be refused! He never returned from camp to civilian life and his years of War service had started.

As a baby, David could have no recollection of his parents first married home, a modern semi in Bramhall on the outskirts of the Manchester conurbation. His mother moved with David back to Cumberland to be near her parents soon after Denis had joined up.

David has some recollection of living in a cottage in Grange in Borrowdale, enough to be able to point it out in later life. He remembers some of the furniture being new then and the nineteen thirties popular records his mother would play on the gramophone. However, his first

11. David and His Mum

vivid memory is of the sale of his grandparents' home at Hazel Bank early in the War. It was a lovely warm day and the furniture was laid out on the lawn for auction. David remembers as a little boy of three thinking, "This is a very sad day." He also remembers being left to stay at a nursery in Keswick for short periods, presumably while his mother went to visit his father. On another occasion, he remembers going with his mother to Leeds to see his father. He has no recollection of his father on this visit but remembers thinking it was nearer to the dangers of the War.

His grandparents retired and moved to a rented bungalow with its garden leading down to the river at Pooley Bridge about one hundred yards from Ullswater Steamer landing stage. David, still only three, and his mother moved to a tiny rented terraced cottage opposite the old bobbin mill in the hamlet of Howtown on Ullswater. It must have been a two-up and two-down house with the earth privy across the grass outside the cottages along a short slate-flagged path. There was a bus service only twice a week into Penrith on market day and Saturday and a summer steamer service at the weekend on the lake to Pooley Bridge and Glenridding. There was no school or shop in Howtown, the centre of the hamlet was the Howtown Hotel, a family inn, which was across the beck from the old bobbin mill which had become the village hall. It would have been a dramatic change in lifestyle for David's mother who had been brought up by parents who were comfortably off hoteliers, she having all she needed, including her own dress account at the leading ladies shop in Keswick and a chauffeur driven car to take her there when she wanted.

12. Howton, Ullswater

However, Howtown was not a quiet place during the War. There was a Commando battle training camp up one of the valleys behind the hamlet. Dances were held in the old bobbin mill village hall. David's mother played the piano at the dances and no doubt did some dancing with the young Commando officers! She also helped at the Howtown Hotel.

David has clear memories as a little boy of three to four free to wander about Howtown, playing by the beck and going on his own down to the lake where the beck flowed in by the steamer landing stage. The water shelved deeply but David remembers being well aware of the danger. Here, he first learnt the pleasure of fishing. His tackle was a jam jar on a long piece of string and initially some bread as bait in the jar. His prey was the minnows which lived in shoals along the lake shore. He quickly learnt the shoal came at once, looking for food, each time something fell in the water. The skill required was to land the jar in the water with its open end facing the oncoming shoal of investigating minnows which stopped to feed on the bread, a few would enter the jar to be quickly pulled out. The catch was then put into another jar to be taken back to the cottage to be fed live to the cat on the slate flag path to the privy. However, the cat had a ferocious appetite for live minnows and David needed to improve his fishing technique to meet demand. He quickly realized the bread bait which spilled out of the jar to some extent prevented a maximum catch. Without the bait and after throwing one stone in the water to ascertain the movement of the shoal, he confidently landed his jar with a good splash with its open end facing the direction in which the shoal had just gone. Sure enough, the shoal swam back straight past the unnoticed jar, many straight into it! The jar for the live minnows was soon packed like sardines, ready to be delivered to the cat! One day a mother and father with their little boy visiting the lake to catch minnows with a very small fine net on the end of a cane complained that David was making so many disturbances in the water that no fish could be caught. When they returned with, as fishermen say, "no luck", David took much pleasure in offering them some of his catch from his stuffed jar. He knew he would soon have it filled up again! There was no such thing as a National Park ranger to take him safely home from the danger of the lake, then to report his mother to the social services department of government for failing to take care of her child. Nor were there do-gooders in those days, who would today have reported him for cruelty to minnows for feeding them live to the cat.

David remembers one day a man asking if Mrs Compston was in. David called to his mother, "There's a man here to see you." She came to the upstairs window to see who it was. It was his father. However, that is all he remembers of that visit from his father!

The Commandos trained in the fells and on the lake. Sometimes David would be taken out on the lake by the officers in their rubber assault craft.

One exercise for the men was to jump into the deep water from the steamer landing stage in full battle kit to swim back to the shore. Little boys love that sort of thing, so David would take up a position on the landing stage to watch. The sergeant in charge would line his men up on the landing stage asking each one before the jump, "Swimmer or non-swimmer?" Any non-swimmers were then relieved of their heavy battle gear, and being attached to a rope, pushed in and hauled back to the shore. On one occasion, the soldier answered, "non-swimmer", and in a flash, had jumped in not to reappear. The sergeant and corporal looking rather alarmed waited long enough for David to start worrying. The sergeant then stripped down to his underpants and dived in for the rescue attempt. As he surfaced, there was a huge outburst of laugher from the shore from those who had already been through the routine. The 'non-swimmer' had swum under water and under the landing stage where he had surfaced to watch his sergeant jump in to rescue him. David never knew what punishment the 'non-swimmer' suffered, but he enjoyed the show!

In 1942, it was decided that David, who was four years old, could go to boarding school. Fyling Hall School from the north Yorkshire coast, ironically just a few miles from where Helga had lived with the Cross family, had evacuated to Cracoe, a beautiful large house on higher ground on the way into Pooley Bridge looking towards the lake and the Lakeland fells. His mother was then freer to spend time with his father who was stationed in Leeds.

Although David's grandparents were living in Pooley Bridge, he only remembers visiting them once when on a school walk to the lake and he was allowed to leave the walk to cross the bridge to see them. Nevertheless, he was happy at Cracoe, proud that when there were outbreaks of flu, German measles and chicken pox, he never fell ill. Perhaps his open-air life at Howtown had made him robust. He would also probably be enjoying the company of children of his own age for the first time in his life.

His mother next moved to a cottage in Finkel Street in Pooley Bridge which had a garden going down to the river. At that time, German prisoners of war were working, clearing the riverbed. David decided he would risk going to meet the enemy and went to the bottom of the garden. They came to say hallo and David remembers going back to his mother and saying they were nice people.

By now, the War was coming to an end and David's mother moved again, this time to Glenridding at the south end of Ullswater. Germany surrendered on 7th May 1945 and the following day, known as VE Day (Victory in Europe), David was given permission to travel in the carrier's van from Cracoe to Glenridding where the flags were out and his mother met him and he had his first ever ice cream as a celebration. In those days, one trusted people and there was no question of the driver not being trusted with the children he took to their home villages: nasty thoughts did not form part of people's makeup at that time. There was no such thing as people requiring some government certificate to show they had been vetted to be allowed to look after children.

His father came home to Glenridding, perhaps for leave. David remembers him being strict and thinking David was extravagant with the jam. To teach him a lesson, he was allocated his ration as was his mother and father. There was no restriction on how much of his ration David could use at each meal, but when it was finished, he was given no more until both his mother and father had used theirs.

Mother moved again, now to a larger house at the end of a drive across a field opposite the village school in Patterdale, a mile or two up the valley from Glenridding. David had broken a leg at Cracoe and was transferred to the village school at Patterdale so he could live at home. Here, as Helga had been when she returned home to go to school, David was bullied by the village boys, but it did him no harm.

David's sister Judith was born in February 1945.

Just after the War ended, his father was demobbed and lived for a short time in Patterdale, taking David to task on wearing out his clothes, probably because he led a robust outdoor life unlike his father's upbringing in central London.

The family then moved to rented rooms in Mellor in Cheshire on the outskirts of the suburbs of Manchester to enable his father to go to his office in Manchester. David could not believe they had come to live on a road with street lights. However, the family soon moved to a cottage next to Townscliffe Farm in Mellor where once again David could go fishing, now using his hands to trap trout under the stones in the steam nearby. Also, he would help on the farm, particularly at haymaking time, turning over the hay in the fields and being put on top of the hay as it was passed up to be stacked in the barn. At an early age, he would even drive the tractor as it worked across the fields being loaded with the hay.

David would have been seven when he first got to know his father. It was not an easy relationship which had got off to a bad start and David never bonded with him but he has very happy memories of life during the War with his mother.

CHAPTER TWO
Peace but Austerity

The War in Europe finished at midnight on 8th May 1945 and four months later it was finally over when Japan surrendered on 2nd September 1945. Although the War had ended these were still very austere times.

Many children had lost fathers, mothers as well as brothers and sisters. Food and clothing were still rationed and in any case, the shops provided limited choice. Toys were in very short supply and very expensive. However, children had learned to enjoy themselves using their imaginations to play games without toys, although they longed for something new to play with. Christmas was a time when such a wish might be met by Father Christmas, but even he had a very limited range! Nevertheless, he always put an orange in the bottom of the stocking and this was a real treat.

Slowly, imported fruit began to appear and for the first time, young children could have a banana. Children's birthday parties were always held at home and were of great fun, of course, with the main treats being jelly and junket. Tomatoes began to be available throughout the year rather than just in the summer. Ice cream was also something new for young children but was made of poor ingredients.

Helga continued her education at Worthington Primary School until she was eleven. During the War years, she feels the teaching was poor; probably many of the female teachers, who seemed old to her, would have gone back into teaching to replace the men and some of the young women teachers who had joined the armed forces. Before the War, and afterwards, most middle-class ladies stopped work when they got married. Perhaps after a few years or more as a housewife, it was quite difficult to return to teaching with certainly no refresher courses provided. There was strict discipline with the use of the cane at times for serious misbehaviour and a sharp rap on the knuckles with a ruler for a lesser misdemeanour. The loos in many schools were outside across the playground.

12. VE Day, Helga and Fiends
(Helga third from right, Alison far right)

Helga loved reading, having to be able to read since she was four, but found mathematics difficult. Teaching focused on 'the three Rs', reading, w'riting and a'rithmetic. She would travel to her godmother, Hilda Brighouse, in Worsley to have French lessons. Miss Brighouse was the sister of Harold Brighouse who was a famous playwright. His plays were on regularly in London, the most well-known being *HOBSON'S CHOICE*, which was made into a film in 1953 staring some of the biggest names in acting of that time. It had been Miss Brighouse who proposed the name "Helga" as the Postlethwaite family name was of Norse origin.

After primary school, Helga went to Sale Secondary Modern School. This was a newly built school and she hated it, still feeling an outsider in suburban Manchester. She and her sister, Alison, joined Brooklands Tennis Club. Her sister, also not an academic, was very good at sport, like their father and was very competitive. Helga remembers when Alison was out quickly at cricket, played on the unmade cul-de-sac drive outside their house, she would go off saying, "I am taking my bat and ball in!" Nevertheless, she went on to play hockey at county level and was a member of the top Manchester athletics club, Sale Harriers. Helga, on the other hand, loved dancing and joined the dancing troop of the Sale Operatic Society when only fourteen, although members were supposed to be over sixteen. There, she met her friend, Edwina Oldham, with whom she kept in touch for the rest of their lives. At that time, there were few professional theatre productions outside London and even though Manchester did boast two big theatres, the twice yearly full scale amateur productions by Sale and other amateur operatic societies were major events attracting full houses throughout the week of their productions. Helga continued to take part as a dancer in these productions until she married and moved away from Sale. It goes without saying that the members of the local rugby clubs would turn up in force for the shows to eye the young ladies taking part.

During Helga's and David's early school years holidays away from home were an exception. Once the War was over, people began to travel for pleasure again, although only infrequently. Very few had cars so travel was by train or service bus. There were practically no coach companies offering tours and certainly no package holidays.

After the War, David and Helga would still be taken for their summer holidays to where they had spent time during the War and sometimes for a week in a caravan near the seaside. Neither David nor Helga enjoyed these caravan holidays as much as returning to where they had been brought up.

On reaching the age of fourteen, Helga decided to travel without her mother or father to Staintondale to stay on the farm with the Cross family. Catching the train at Sale to Manchester, she crossed the city to meet her cousin Colin on his way from college in Wales on the train going to York, where they changed for the train to Scarborough and changed again for Staintondale. There was still the full network of main and branch lines which made it possible to go by train very near to any final destination in England. She decided travelling on her own was better than with her mother when the last time they took the wrong train and finished up in Newcastle!

At fifteen, Helga left school to attend the private Aslett's Secretarial College in Altrincham. There, she met her friend, Pat Holmes, with whom she kept in touch for the rest of their lives. The college was required to teach 'the three Rs' but specialised in teaching bookkeeping, typing and shorthand. Shorthand was a standard part of office procedure being a method for a secretary to make accurate word-by-word notes of the dictation of her boss at the rate of one hundred and twenty words a minute, from which the typed version was produced.

At sixteen, Helga took her first job as a typist at McDougal's, a paint manufacturer in Broadheath, Altrincham, at a salary of £3 per week.

David was far more fortunate than Helga in relation to the

diversity and quality of his education. For a year after the Compston's moved to Mellor, David attended a small private school about a mile from Townscliffe Cottage. He walked to school on his own each day, including throughout the exceptionally snowy winter of 1947.

However, a big change was about to take place in David's education. His father had served in the army with Eric Swain who had been a master at St Hugh's School in Woodhall Spa in Lincolnshire and returned there after he was demobbed. The friendship between David's father and Eric resulted in St Hugh's being chosen as David's prep school, the plan being for him to go on to Mill Hill School in north London. Mill Hill was mainly a boarding all boys' public school (which means it was a privately owned school) where David's father, his uncle Tym and his great uncle Jack had attended. Jack had been senior monitor (head boy) and was killed in the last day of the First World War, only weeks after leaving school.

David was very happy at St Hugh's. He travelled to school at the beginning of terms and back home at the end of terms on his own by steam train. In those days, there was still the "boat train" service between Harwich and Liverpool which had been running since the great migration of people from central Europe to America after the First World War. David's trunk containing all his clothes for the term would be sent by rail a few days in advance to arrive at the school before term started, having been delivered by the railway company from the station at Woodhall Spa. David's father would take him to Dinting station on the outskirts of Manchester to put him on the boat train to Lincoln. There, David would join other boys and a teacher to continue the train journey to Woodhall Spa, changing at Woodhall Junction. Sadly, David's father chose the time on the way to Dinting to criticise David over his last term's school report. It was certainly not the time to do that and it resulted in a further strain in David's relationship with his father. Towards the end of his time at St Hugh's, once or twice his mother and father would drive to Woodhall to pick David up at the end of term, they now being the proud owners of a new car.

The Petwood Hotel in Woodhall Spa had been the officers' mess of the Dambusters during the Second World War. There were several other good hotels in this charming Edwardian town, with its famous golf course and large public park, including a swimming pool. The town was like a little holiday resort which had been popular with Royalty between the wars.

David loved sport and was good at Maths and Geography. He was poor at English and French, although quite good at Latin. Later in life, he realised he was to some degree dyslexic, which was not recognised in those days and no doubt hampered him in learning language subjects. History, he found a bore. Nevertheless, St Hugh's was a very well-appointed school with a good teaching staff. David remembers with appreciation the physical training master. He was appropriately named Sergeant Rawe. Having been brought up by his mother, who was inclined to be nervous, David needed to gain confidence and he credits Sergeant Rawe with giving him this, through teaching him to climb ropes, boxing and swimming. He also taught woodwork, a skill David utilised for the rest of his life. There were excellent sports facilities including a large playing field laid out with many cricket pitches in the summer and rugby and soccer in the winter and spring, an outdoor swimming pool, gymnasium, tennis courts and even a .22 rifle range. As a senior, David was in the school first XV and a school prefect.

The headmaster, Mr Forbes, owned the school and was a

jovial character of Irish background. His wife, on the other hand, was a typical schoolma'am.

There was a strong Church of England influence with the whole school attending church each Sunday in the town, a short walk from school. Twice a term there would be exeats after Sunday church when boys could go home until the early evening service in the gym. Living so far away, David usually stayed in school, except when he had been invited by a local family for the day.

During the winter and spring terms, Mr Forbes would put on a Saturday film evening in the gym. There would be a documentary and a main feature, usually a war or adventure film; a particular favourite was the film of the airborne landing and attack on the bridge at Arnhem. Many years later, this epic battle was retold in the film, *A BRIDGE TOO FAR*.

Discipline was good but not too strict. For serious breaches of discipline, there would be a caning from the headmaster in his study, 'six of the best!' It always seemed to involve a group of boys who had been up to some prank together. Lining up outside the study, the boys would wait, expecting the worst. However, there was the ploy of putting a book down the back of one's trousers in the hope that Mr Forbes would not notice as he applied the cane to the book rather than the bottom. Of course, he did notice but pretended not to, having achieved his objective by simply calling the boys to his study to be punished by only hurting their egos, not their bottoms!

State education was organised with primary schooling until eleven, then there was the "eleven-plus exam". Those that passed, went on to grammar school, the others to secondary modern. Although St Hugh's, being a private school, did not prepare the boys for the eleven-plus, David did come home to take the exam at the local school in Mellor. He never knew if he passed!

David loved rugby and was in the 1st XV in his last year. In those days, the only school team in each sport was the first team in the final year. David also enjoyed soccer, played in the spring term and cricket in the summer term, but did not make the school teams in either.

In February 1952, David's last year at St Hugh's, King George VI died and Queen Elizabeth II came to the throne. All the school attended the proclamation of the new Queen in the town read out by the

14. Three Queens at HM George VI's funeral

Leader of the Council. At Helga's college, the principal entered the classroom, asking for silence, as he announced, "The King is dead." The BBC stopped all programmes and played solemn music for the rest of the day.

At the end of the summer term, David left to go to Mill Hill, settling in very quickly and finding school records of his great-uncle Jack, including the team photograph with him as captain of the 1916 first XV. David's housemaster in Ridgeway House, Major Bush, had won the Military Cross at the battle of Arnhem and his house tutor, Mr 'Ted' Winter, was a Cumbrian having played county rugby for Cumberland and Westmorland. Most of the masters had served as officers in the army in the War. There was still food rationing, which included sweets, although this came to an end while David was at Mill Hill.

Friends were quickly made including Tim Adamson, whose father had been at Mill Hill at the same time as David's. David left after only one term in the lower sixth form. This was no doubt due to the beginning of the breakdown of his parents' marriage, his father now planning a

15. Jim's high Specification sports bike

new life. David's uncle Sandy Badrock had taken over the Scafell Hotel in Borrowdale from his parents and invited Tim and David to holiday there which involved rock climbing with Sandy. Tim became a very competent rock climber. Sadly, he died while still in his twenties. Part of David's school summer holidays each year were spent with his uncle at the Scafell Hotel, the other part with the family at his grandparents who had retired to Pooley Bridge on Ullswater.

16. Serious rock climbing. David leads.

David's closest friend at Mill Hill was Jim Kent. They have remained very close friends throughout life. At school, they played together in the school teams, David captaining the school junior colts and colts XVs. Jim would join David for the week at the Scafell Hotel in their last year or two at Mill Hill. Jim and he competed for a top place in Maths, Jim just having the edge. They were members of the Young Farmers Club and kept hens and ducks, making pocket money selling eggs and ducks at Christmas. David was 'fag' in his first year to Jim's older brother, Ben. A fag had to undertake chores for his fag-master, such as cleaning shoes and preparing a hot drink after prep in the evening. Ben has also remained a friend after they left school.

17. David and Jim reach the top

Discipline in house was run on rather military grounds with most of the control delegated to the prefects. It worked well in a system where there was much respect shown to one's seniors.

David did reasonably well in class, though not well enough to please his father. His strong subjects continued to include Maths, Art and Geography and now Physics. He was weaker at English, Chemistry and History, although passed at O level in all these subjects. French, he failed in. He gave up Latin to be able to study Art and History of Art, winning the senior Art prize in his last summer term. This decision to give up Latin was one his housemaster tried to persuade him not to make, as Latin was required for entrance to Oxford or Cambridge at that time. Nevertheless, the subjects taken were the right foundation for the career David chose.

One experience left a deep impression on David. Although playing front row in school rugby teams, being the right build for such a position and certainly not the fastest player on the field, he was a good kicker and took the goal kicks. His year in Ridgeway House had most of the school team scrum, but no one competent to play in the backs. Burton Bank, one of the other houses, had a good spread of the school XV in the year senior to David's. In the house competitions, David played at fly half, where his kicking could be used to avoid the ball reaching the very weak three-quarters. While still in the under-fifteen junior colts, David's house Ridgeway reached the final of the under-sixteen house rugby competition to face the older and better-balanced Burton Bank team. A senior boy from another house took on the challenge of team manager for Ridgeway. He planned that Ridgeway could dominate the forward play, using David at fly half to simply keep kicking for touch, making sure the ball was never passed to his three-quarters. One could kick straight into touch to gain ground in those days. These tactics were followed absolutely. In what must have been the most boring game of rugby to watch, there was no scoring until near the end when David found touch near the Burton Bank line and from there the Ridgeway scrum fought over the line for a try to win the match. This was a lesson in management planning and discipline which David remembered and applied to his professional career. Manchester United's Sir Alex Ferguson was, of course, the past master of such management.

However, David's school days were to finish after only one term in the lower sixth form. He left Mill Hill at Christmas in 1955, having achieved his ambition of being in the first XV and gaining his colours. Leaving school before completing the two years in the sixth form prevented David from taking A-level exams and therefore going to university. Tim kept David informed of the goings-on at Mill Hill writing long letters, including one covering the fire in the science block.

During Helga and David's schooldays, life was still austere. Coal provided the major source of energy to power practically all industry at that time, to generate electricity and to provide heating by open fires in the home. Gas was produced from coal and known as "town gas" being produced locally in the larger towns and cities, and being piped to homes and public buildings for cooking. All this reliance on coal made the atmosphere dirty. Office workers all wore white shirts which had removable collars and cuffs which at the end of the day were so dirty from the grime in the atmosphere that they were replaced for the next day. The grime covered buildings and the stone walls on the hills between Lancashire and Yorkshire. There was frequent fog referred to as "smog." Visibility could be down to five yards, practically making driving impossible, one could even walk into a post in front of you! Thus, the song, *A FOGGY DAY IN LONDON TOWN*, became popular.

However, in the mid1950s, The Clean Air Act began to change things by requiring coal to be replaced by smokeless fuel in open fires. Initially, it applied to city centres; the impact was quite dramatic. Driving with great difficulty in smog into the city through the suburbs; on reaching the city centre, one suddenly came into bright sunshine. In time, the controls on the use of coal in all built-up areas was banned.

However, the years were now in sight which were described by Prime Minister Harold Macmillan as, "You have never had it so good." Post-War austerity was coming to an end.

CHAPTER THREE
Into the World of Work

In 1952, Helga started work cycling each day, six days a week between Sale Moor and Broadheath, about three miles. Saturdays were half working days in what was the standard fourty-four-hour working week for office workers. She was paid £3 per week as a shorthand typist at McDougall, household decorating materials supplies.

She continued to live with her parents in Sale Moor at 10 Warwick Drive, a typical 1930s semi in a cul-de-sac. The house had an attractive entrance into a hall with staircase, a sitting room, dining room and kitchen, each with access to the hall and a back kitchen. Upstairs, there were two double bedrooms and a small single with a family bathroom and separate toilet. Outside, there was a small garden.

The house was heated with coal fires, all the downstairs rooms, the two double bedrooms and the kitchen had fireplaces. All this was typical of the time. Nevertheless, normally only the kitchen and sitting room fires would be lit. Very few houses had central heating. Cooking was by gas, although the kitchen range with the coal fire and oven could be used.

Very few houses had TV and there was only BBC until ITV started in 1955. Families had their favourite programmes on radio which they would gather round to hear each week, *FRIDAY NIGHT IS MUSIC NIGHT*, with a big London band or orchestra with one or two singers, Joe Loss and Ted Heath were the top band conductors.

On Sunday, there was The Palm Court Orchestra with Max Jaffa from Scarborough. The Musicians' Union was strong enough to limit the BBC from regularly playing records.

There were three radio broadcasting programmes transmitted by the BBC, The Home Service, which covered news and middle of the road music with some plays, The Light Programme which covered pop music of the day, again played live by bands from London and a few of the big cities such as Manchester, as well as live sport commentaries. Also, The Light Programme had some other entertainment, such as *THE ARCHERS* – a story of country folk and Helga's favourite on Saturday mornings, *DICK BARTON SPECIAL AGENT*. On records, American big band music and singers were very popular with teenagers and young people. The best British big bands were Ted Heath and His Orchestra in London and the arguably even better, the BBC Northern Dance Orchestra in Manchester, with conductor Alan Ainsworth.

The other BBC transmission was the Third Programme of highbrow classical music. All BBC broadcasts finished at midnight with the epilogue, sometimes read by Helga's uncle, Frank Drake, followed by the national anthem.

Radio Luxembourg broadcast from Europe in English playing the top pop records of the day, but reception was poor. Nevertheless, young people tuned in, especially for its version of the top twenty records late on Sunday night. In November 1952 the *NEW MUSICAL EXPRESS* first drew up its own Top Twelve from a random twenty out of fifty-two stores willing to send in sales figures. However these were sales of sheet music, not record singles. It was not until 1955, when other musical periodicals started up rival charts, that there was the switch-over from sheet music to actual discs. Once the *NEW MUSICAL EXPRESS* had established its *TOP TWENTY*, Radio

Luxembourg use it for its broadcasts on Sunday night.

Helga's parents, like the majority at the time, did not have a phone until about 1954. All phones were rented from the GPO, the General Post Office. Once ordered, it took months before one was received. Many were on a party line shared by a neighbour, only one could use it at a time and if one lifted the phone to make a call when the neighbour was on the line, one could hear the other conversation.

Money was in pounds, shillings and pence (£.s.d). Twelve pence to the shilling and twenty shillings to the pound. The smallest denomination was a quarter of a penny known as a farthing.

Helga paid her mother £2 of her £3 per week original salary, increasing the payment to mother as her salary increased.

Nevertheless, from starting work, Helga became free to establish a social life without her mother's influence. She continued to be very active in the dancing troop of the Sale Operatic Society, which did two productions a year, mainly musicals that had finished their professional runs in London and New York a few years earlier. These included *CAROUSEL* and other smash hits before they became Hollywood blockbuster films.

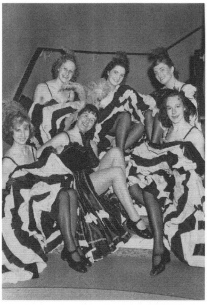

18. Helga dances Helga top right

Helga played tennis with her father and sister in the Sale Public Park and then with Alison, joined a small local tennis club before moving 'upmarket' to the Brooklands Tennis Club. David played rugby at Ashton-on-Mersey. There was a very active social scene which linked the activities of the tennis club with those of Sale Rugby and Ashton-on-Mersey Rugby clubs. All rugby union was amateur, Sale being a top club had a number of internationals in their team. Drug taking in sport, or that matter for recreation, was unheard of at that time in the UK. For a rugby union player, the most serious offence was to play with, or even train with, rugby league players. To do so could lead to a ban on playing rugby union in the future.

19. David plays rugby (David seated centre)

At weekends, there would be club disco type dances run by the members themselves, known as "hops." While Sale Rugby Club did not hold events on Friday nights, in view of taking the games on Saturday very seriously, Aston-on-Mersey Rugby Club put fun as its priority and became recognised as the 'in' place for young people. Once a month in the autumn and winter, Ashton-on-Mersey

Rugby Club held a Friday night dance in the Stanford Hall ballroom in Altrincham, one of the largest in England. The music was provided by Alan Ainsworth and his full big band, the BBC Northern Dance Orchestra. The singers were pop record stars of the day. Every month, the dance was completely sold out in advance. Tickets were £1 and, needless to say, there would always be Sale rugby players there. On each Saturday night in winter, Ashton-on-Mersey would hold 'hops', that were so well-known that players from top London teams visiting Manchester would finish up there. The girlfriends would produce freshly cooked food after the matches. Chips in plenty, prepared after peeling the potatoes, were cooked on an old electric stove in the old army wooden hut which was the club house. Frozen chips and health and safety were unheard of. In summer, cellar parties would take place in houses where the parents were away. Skiffle and guitar music were just coming on the scene with a few friends able to provide live music at these parties. In all, it was a very active and fun social scene for the young people of south Manchester/ North Cheshire.

Very few families had cars and favourite boyfriends were the 'travelling reps,' a posh name for salesmen, who had small company cars. Some others had 'bangers', mostly pre-War cars in poor repair and not really fit for the road. However, there was not much traffic in the evenings and late at night. There was certainly

ROCK 'N ROLL . . . THE CELLAR STYLE

20. Rock 'n' Roll – The Cellar Style
(Helga back right)

too much drinking and driving, however, in the unusual event of being stopped by the police, one was considered fit to drive if one could walk in a straight line for about ten yards at the police station!

Helga had her twenty-first birthday party at the fashionable ballroom of The Royal George Hotel in Knutsford, hosted by her parents, with a small resident band playing for the dancing. There was nothing special about eighteenth birthdays in those days.

HELGA'S 21ˢᵗ BIRTHDAY PORTRAIT

21. Helga's 21st Birthday

Most records were sold on the brittle 78 rpm material, but vinyl 45 rpm and 33 rpm long-playing records were now on the market, but expensive. There were popular public dance halls, there were no reputable night clubs, and the young people in Helga and David's social group preferred the private sports club dances and 'hops'. Rock and Roll was just coming in. Helga and friends decorated a cellar where one of their cellar parties even received favourable press coverage.

David, being a little over two and a half years younger than Helga, entered the world of work straight from school in January 1956. By this time, Helga was well into working life and had an active social life.

During the year leading up to David leaving school, David's father focused David's attention on what was to be his job in life. His father being a chartered accountant considered a profession appropriate.

Various brochures from the professional bodies were produced, excluding, of course, those that required a university education such as medicine.

Included were those of the Institutions of Mechanical, Electrical and Civil Engineering. David felt confident he could do well in engineering and wanted to be a civil engineer, seeing himself designing roads, bridges, dams and ports. He did not like the idea of being involved in power stations.

Accordingly, David's father arranged for David to become a trainee engineer under article agreement with the Chief Engineer of the Manchester Ship Canal Company, the UK's third largest port on the basis of tonnage handled per year. The training period was for five years, with 'day release' to attend college once a week in term-time for the first two years. David joined the part-time course in Municipal Engineering at the Manchester College of Science and Technology, MCS&T (later to become UMIST, the University of Manchester Institute of Science and Technology).

In years one and two, there were lectures on one day a week and one day a week evening lectures between six thirty p.m. and eight p.m. In the last three years, all lectures were in the evening, known as night school. Some of the lecturers were professors from the University of Manchester which was associated to MCS&T, others were working in industry. Indeed, some of David's colleagues in the design office at the Ship Canal Company lectured at MCS&T.

The course in Municipal Engineering was recognised by the Institution of Civil Engineers as equal to a university degree in civil engineering with one addition subject to be taken separately. David did this by going to Salford College on a fourth night each week in his last year.

David was inspired by LTC Rolt's biographies of the early engineers, Thomas Telford, the canal, roads and bridges engineer, as well as the famous railway engineers, George and Robert Stephenson and Isambard Kingdom Brunel. The construction of the Manchester Ship Canal ranked with the achievements of these famous engineers. By now, David had developed an ambition to have a challenging and creative engineering career.

By the summer of 1960, David had passed all the exams to become a graduate of the Institution of Civil Engineers, the same status as a BSc. David considers those five years of training and study could not have been a better foundation for his professional career. He must thank his father for the guidance he gave.

He started work in 1956 in the Ship Canal design office in King Street in the centre of Manchester. He first had to make the tea and learn to hand print very tidily, before being involved in producing simple engineering drawings by tracing from sketches produced by the engineers in the office.

Working on a large drawing board, these drawings were usually done in ink on special semi-transparent linen sheets from which copies could be made on a special print machine. Blue prints had been superseded by this time. Sometimes the less-important drawings were done on large sheets of tracing paper which were vulnerable to damage in storage.

The management of David's training under articles was delegated by the Chief Engineer to Mr Oswald Hardy, the Deputy Chief Engineer.

Mr Hardy had previously worked for a leading London-based international consulting engineers, Coude and Partners. Mr Hardy took a close interest in David's training, ensuring he established a sound grounding in civil engineering design and excellent site experience.

By the end of his training period, David had designed various port installations, including the lower leading jetty at Latchford Locks near Warrington. This design was submitted by David to the Institution of Civil Engineers as part of the procedure to become a chartered engineer.

He had also worked on several sites, including being resident engineer on jetty construction, major earthworks and a large span steel pipe bridge over the River Mersey. As resident engineer, David had authority over the contractors to ensure the works were carried out to specification, as well as approving all payments to the contractors.

22. Lower leading jetty at Latchford Locks

In short, by the time David finished his training with the Ship Canal Company, he had all the experience he needed to submit himself for professional interview to the Institution of Civil Engineers to become a chartered engineer. The only obstacle was his age. One could not take the interview until twenty-four and if passed, could not take up the status of professional engineer, AMICE, until twenty-five. David was still only twenty-two.

23. Thelwall Pipe Bridge

He vowed to himself that since he had not been to university and obtained a degree but had a much wider experience than those of the same age now just graduating, but without practical experience, that he would never let any graduate colleague of his and of the same age get ahead of him in work or seniority.

However, David's focus on his professional career resulted in his rugby having to take second place to work and study. Although on leaving school he joined Broughton Park Rugby Club, a first-class club with international players, he found he could not find the time for the fitness training to compete for a place in the first XV. He decided to join Ashton on Mersey where his college friend, Bill

Hoskinson, played. This move proved to be one of the deciding moments in his life, as it was through Ashton on Mersey Rugby Club, that he met Helga. Meanwhile David's friend, Jim Kent, had an outstanding rugby career, playing at first for the Old Millhillians, at that time one of the leading London clubs with international players. Jim played county rugby for Middlesex when they won the county championship, as well as playing for London Home Counties and being selected as a reserve for England.

David's period of study and practical experience was set against a thriving industrial and construction period in the North West. James Drake (later Sir James) was designing and building the UK's first motorway, the M6 round Preston. He had the splendid title of Lancashire County Surveyor and Bridgemaster. In Trafford Park, Metropolitan Vickers were manufacturing some of the largest turbines and transformers for power stations at home and aboard. At Woodford in Cheshire, A V Roe were designing the next generation of the jet long-range bomber, the Vulcan. Also in Cheshire, Ilford was making film in competition with the American giant, Kodak. In Stockport, Mather & Platt were manufacturing textile machines for the still thriving cotton and woollen industry in the UK, as well as exporting them. Shipbuilding was still a major industry on Merseyside and Barrow in Furness. Professor Lovell was busy designing and building the world's first radio telescope at Jodrell Bank in Cheshire. Manchester University and its associated College of Science and Technology were at the heart of all this engineering and manufacturing activity. For those entering the world of work at this time, there were plenty of options in the context of full employment and a well-balanced UK economy.

The police were still unarmed. The "British Bobby", as policemen were known, relied on policing by respect and consent, rather than the point of a gun.

In 1957, the era of space communication started with the launch of the Russian satellite, Sputnik 1. Very few people in those days appreciated how space technology was to change life in the years ahead, leading to mass communication shared by all the world's population.

In the 1950s and 60s, there was mass immigration from Commonwealth countries to the UK. Workers from the Caribbean came in large numbers to play their part in rebuilding the post-war urban London economy, fulfilling labour requirements in hospitals and the transport system. They spoke English, were Christians, loved cricket, were cheerful and had music which was appreciated by the indigenous British population.

Also, there was mass immigration from India and Pakistan. The Indians proved to be socioeconomically affluent and became part of the middle class. Their religion did not impact on British culture. The Pakistanis helped to resolve the labour shortages in the British steel and textile industries, while many establishing businesses in retail. The majority were Muslims. This first wave of Pakistanis, like those from the Caribbean, spoke English, loved cricket and integrated well into British society, particularly in the industrial areas of the Midlands and the North of England.

However, such was the rate of this immigration from the Commonwealth, that Acts of Parliament were passed in 1962 and 1971 which largely restricted further primary immigration from the old Empire. Nevertheless, over the years ahead there continued to be an ever increasing proportion of the population of the Islamic faith, not just from the Indian subcontinent, but also from the Middle East. Sadly, at the time of writing, it has become clear that the cultural differences between the indigenous Christian population and those of the Islamic faith were leading to tensions in society in some parts of the country.

A proportion of the immigrants did not even speak or understand English. Political and religious strife in the Himalayan Region and the Middle East was acting as a catalyst for a very small minority of those of the Islamic faith and extreme views to disrupt the vision of a peaceful multicultural society in the UK by partaking in acts of terrorism.

CHAPTER FOUR
St Valentine Intervenes

With Helga's urge to 'spread her wings,' she made a move to work in central Manchester after about two and a half years of working in Broadheath. A short walk to Sale station with an easy commute by electric train took her to the centre of town where she worked for Shannon Systems in St James's Square, office materials and equipment suppliers. She worked under the lady office manager, who seemed to be off work very often looking after her mother.

Helga's tasks covered bookkeeping, including doing the wages and working out the commissions due to each of the salesmen, there being about twelve of them. She remembers them as a very likable lot, most of them had fought in the War. In addition, she acted as a secretary and shorthand typist. She worked there for about six years. By the end of this time, 1961, she was paid £6 per week and decided to leave when she was refused a ten shilling a week rise.

Although David and Helga had met each other at the same 'hops' and dances from time to time, it was at the Sale Rugby Club's St Valentine's fancy dress 'hop' pyjama party on 14th February 1959 that David became her 'white knight' and took her home at the end of the evening. She decided the boy who she had arranged to meet there had overplayed his cards when he and his friend walked into the bar both wearing a nappy, very correctly arranged, using large terry towels and big safety pins. Nevertheless, David and Helga remained friends with 'Jungle' Green, the nappy man. He had served in the army fighting in the jungles of Malaya. David shared a flat with him when David decided it was time to 'fly the nest'. The Friday night after the St Valentine's fancy dress pyjama party was the date for the Manchester Ship Canal Company Annual Dinner Dance attended by the chairman of the company and the Lord Mayor of Manchester. It was a splendid occasion when David could wear his 'white tie and tails'.

This was to be the first time David would ask Helga out. However, he was very upset when she said she could not go for the very good reason that her sister, Alison, was getting married the next day, and, as was to be expected, Helga would be her chief bridesmaid. David took Helga's best friend, Liz Smith, to the Ship Canal dinner dance instead!

However, this inauspicious start to the relationship was quickly overcome when the next Friday, Helga agreed to go with David to the Ashton on Mersey Rugby Club dance at the Stanford Hall in Altrincham where Alan Ainsworth and the BBC Northern Dance Orchestra were playing as usual for these 'sellout' rugby dances.

In the summer of 1959, Helga had her first holiday abroad with her friend Anne. They took the train to London, Anne's mother giving them £5 each at the station when she saw them off. In those days, flying was quite special; most people had not flown. The captains were all dashing young men who had been fighter or bomber pilots in the War. If one was flying British Airways, one could check in at the Cromwell Road Air Terminal in West London from where one was taken by coach to the boarding area for the flight.

In Paris, Helga and Anne had been booked into a somewhat downmarket hotel in 'the red-light district'! Helga says it was a garret! Their eyes were quickly opened to 'life in the city'. The hotel was near Folies Bergere, but they did not go, they could not afford it. They made the most of their time walking everywhere and visiting all the important sights but did not go shopping.

14. Helga in Paris… need one say more!

David took his holiday with his old schoolfriend, Jim Kent, cycling all the way to the Lake District from Cheshire, to stay with David's Uncle Sandy at their family's hotel, the Scafell Hotel in Rosthwaite in Borrowdale. David's grandparents had the hotel before Sandy took over.

David's parents moved from their small rather depressing Victorian mill worker's semi in Mellor to a splendid house in Marple called "Woodstock". David's twenty-first birthday was in October

1959. It had been a long, dry summer with no rain between early April until after David's birthday. Water had to be collected from standpipes in the street and toilets flushed with washing-up water. Nevertheless, David's parents put on a splendid party attended by the rugby and tennis crowd from Sale. Soon after, David's father left home. It was the start of the break-up of the marriage with divorce to take place quickly. David's mother with his granny moved to Woodford in Cheshire with Judith, who was still only fourteen and attending boarding school in Cumbria. She had been close to her father but sadly, his leaving home and showing up to take Judith out from school with the lady he was now living with, resulted in an uneasy relationship thereafter. David decided it was time to 'fly the nest' and moved to Sale first to a 'bedsit' then to share a flat with 'Jungle' Green, the 'nappy' man.

25. "Woodleigh"   *26. "Woodstock"*

David had acquired an 'old banger' while at the Ship Canal Company, his company car having to be given up when the work he was supervising on site was completed. It was a 1939 Flying Standard 9, becoming affectionately known as 'FMP', the letters of its registration number. New, it would have been to a high specification with leather seats and a sunshine roof. The gearbox/clutch was excellent, changing gear was like using an electric switch. The brakes were cable type and were awful, continuously needing adjustment. By now, the sunshine roof leaked. This was repaired using a greased tape, Denso Tape. David and Helga repainted the car grey.

Helga started to learn to drive in 'FMP'. With a maximum speed of thirty-one mph, a trip was made in 'FMP' with two friends to Scotland, calling in Borrowdale on the way. On the way back, while going through Carlisle over the cobbledstone streets, there was a strong smell of petrol. David asked Helga to hold onto the door so it could be opened very quickly if the car caught fire, while continuing to drive out of town, where he would find the fault and repair it! It turned out to be a cracked copper fuel line where it entered the carburettor. A bit was cut off and the line reconnected. The journey continued along Ullswater and over Kirkstone Pass, David advising his passengers they may have to get out and walk if it proved too steep for 'FMP'! However, now with an improved fuel flow, 'FMP' made it to the top!

As David and Helga's courtship developed, after Friday or Saturday nights out, they would take 'FMP' and park in Fairy Lane which was a rough stone lane leading from the edge of Sale Moor through a wood to Priory Park where Helga's great-uncle, Sir Edwin Stockton, had once lived. Parked in Fairy Lane, David and Helga began to realise how much they had in common. They talked about being brought up in the country, Helga in north Yorkshire, David in Cumberland. They both wanted to move out of suburbia and began to dream of where they would live together if they got married. That quiet spot in Fairy Lane is now on a ten-lane section of the M62 south Manchester motorway ring road!

Parking one Sunday in a viewing lay-by one of 'FMP's' front wheels failed to turn with the other. On inspection, it was determined that the locking pin holding the universal joint to the steering rod had sheared. A spare part would be too expensive. So, this was soon put right using a bent nail! Then one afternoon while driving home to Marple David heard a large explosion from 'FMP's' engine followed by a smell of burning oil. One of the pistons had shot out of the side of the engine casting. Was this the end of dear old 'FMP' that was much needed for David's social and love life? No, the garage in Marple would fit a brass patch to the engine casting and fit a new piston. However, towards the end of summer, Helga was driving back from the rugby club with her L-plates on under David's instruction, when David said, "Can't you keep driving straight!?" To which, Helga replied, "It won't go straight." On stopping, it was established a front wheel was falling off. It was time to get rid of 'FMP'. There was no MOT test for cars. It sold for £12 and ran for many more years!

Society at that time was quite disciplined, perhaps the discipline needed in the War years lingered on. The police were still completely unarmed, except for a truncheon, the criminal fraternity likewise did not carry firearms.

Family was the centre of society; based on marriage. Children were expected to be brought into the world by married parents. Those that were unlucky enough to be born to unmarried parents were regarded as illegitimate and known as "bastards", which was certainly very unkind and unfair, since they were in no way responsible for their unhappy status in society.

To be divorced was very frowned upon and could even compromise one's status and progress up the ladder of promotion at work. To live unmarried with another of the opposite sex was to be 'living in sin'. Practicing homosexuals were breaking the law although lesbians were not. The word 'gay' had no sexual connotation, being in common use to describe being merry, light-hearted or showy.

The contraceptive pill was soon to appear but the 'permissive society' was a long way into the future.

Nevertheless, young people were, as throughout time, looking to establish a happy and rewarding life. Men were considered the 'breadwinners' in a family. Most upper- and middle-class girls saw their role in life to marry, help create a comfortable home and bring children into the world, staying at home as a housewife and mother to look after the children as they grew up.

Pop music of the day focused on love and romance, as young people yearned for a happy and lasting relationship with the opposite sex in the context of marriage. Consequently, as two young people began to see the potential for their future together, they would start courting, looking for time together with some privacy, in the park, behind the haystack, or for those with a car, down a quiet country lane.

To propose marriage was the man's prerogative, except on 29th February in a leap year. Being engaged was a serious matter, for if one decided to break off the engagement, one could be taken to court for 'breach of promise' and required to pay damages to one's former fiancé.

Although Helga had had several boyfriends, as indeed David had had several girlfriends, none were serious. Now, when David and Helga were seen together at the rugby club, their friends observed it was different this time. They had fallen wildly in love.

When David completed his articled training with the Ship Canal at the end of 1960, he decided he needed a short spell doing reinforced concrete design before moving on in his career, hoping to work overseas. He applied to C. S. Allott & Son who at the time were about to move from central Manchester to a larger office in Sale. Little did he know, he was joining the second longest established consulting engineers in the world with a history which linked directly to the great Victorian engineers, George and Robert Stephenson, of whom he had read and admired as role models for the engineering profession. He stayed with the company for the rest of his career, mainly involved in the planning, design and construction management of power stations. He never did much reinforced concrete design.

By the time David joined C. S. Allott & Son in January 1961, Helga had her responsible job at Shannon Systems in Manchester. She had always been a supportive daughter in the home, house-proud and being involved in keeping the house clean while her mother's priority was her work in textiles sales based in Manchester and travelling to customers. Helga's sister, Alison, was some two years younger and married just before she was twenty-one to David Wilford. He was a merchant naval officer working for the famous Cunard Line. Cunard at that time provided the passenger service between Southampton and New York. David served as first officer on the *QUEEN MARY*. Jet travel was still to become a norm.

For David and Helga, 1960 was the year of, as the song in the musical SOUTH PACIFIC put it, "getting to know you, getting to know all about you." They arranged to go to Norway for a week in September. Sailing from Newcastle on the Fred Olsen Line to Bergen, it was a rough crossing with one night on board. David and Helga were given cabins on different decks. There was to be no misbehaving allowed on the Fred Olsen Line! Helga's cabin was for six berths and was in the bowels of the ship with no window or porthole and the continuous thud of the engine. The steel door crashed close like a prison. Sharing with a Norwegian lady who snored, Helga left the cabin and went up to the saloon and slept in a chair there.

They stayed in separate rooms in a charming hotel near the waterfront in Bergen. They thought Bergen was lovely. After a few days, they decided to take the Bergen to Oslo train up to Voss where they stayed and from where they took a bus down to Flam on the Hardanger Fjord for a sail along the fjord. It was a beautiful and dramatic drive down the very steep road to Flam. On returning home, family and friends expected them to be engaged, but that was to be a little further in the future, as David was only twenty-two and Helga was twenty-four and a half.

People got married quite young at that time. Coming up to Helga's birthday in March 1961, David went out and bought an emerald and diamond engagement ring. He proposed in the flat he shared with 'Jungle' Green just before her birthday and she said "Yes!" In addition, David gave her *GOOD HOUSEKEEPING'S PICTURE RECIPES* and a hand whisk, both of which she still had and used more than fifty years later. She had a wooden trunk in her bedroom where she kept things for when she got married. Helga was saving up and told her mother she would pay for the wedding herself.

That summer, Uncle Sandy invited David and Helga to go with him to Connemara in Southern Ireland. They were to meet him at Stranraer for the ferry to Larne in Northern Ireland. David and Helga took the night sleeper train from Manchester to Stranraer. They were allocated sleeper cabins at opposite ends of the coach with the sleeping car attendant having his cabin between them. Like Fred Olsen Line, British Railways was not going to allow any misbehaving! From Stranraer, they drove in Sandy's car to Connemara. Uncle Sandy was to stay at the Ballynahinch Castle

Hotel salmon fishing. David and Helga stayed in Clifton for the first night. Once again, Helga landed unlucky with her accommodation. The bed in her room was dirty with a cigarette end and cigarette holder in it! The next day, they moved to Roundstone with, of course, separate rooms. Checking out after a few days, the receptionist asked them to work out their bill! Well, this was Ireland! The last day and night was spent at the Ballynahinch Castle giving David and Helga a day to salmon fish with Sandy.

Just before David joined C. S. Allott & Son, the company had been appointed by the Central Electricity Generating Board (CEGB) to design and supervise the construction of a proposed 2,000 megawatt (MW) coal-fired Ferrybridge 'C' Power Station, which was to become one of the largest in the world. The company had a long history in power station design and construction going back to the turn of the century. Their projects had included Battersea and Croydon power stations which at that time provided London with most of its electricity. All the power stations in Manchester and the north-west were Allott stations.

27. Ferry bridge 'C' Power Station

Consequently, the firm's partners and small group of senior staff had wide experience for the task ahead. Nevertheless, there was an urgent need to increase the staff numbers. David was fortunate to be one of the first of this staff build-up, joined quickly by his friend Bill Hoskinson, who had just finished his training with the City of Manchester Highways Department. David was given the task of working with the project engineer, Dick Bower, to plan the layout of the power station, while Bill worked on the diversion of the main road that crossed where the power station was to be built.

The CEGB decided that construction must start on site in September 1961, and it was now April. The first contract was for site preparation which involved major earthworks to level the site for all the many buildings, the drainage systems for surface and foul water, the roads round the future power station buildings with underground service ducts for cable systems to be installed later, together with the diversion of the main road which crossed the site. The build-up of staff had barely started.

However, David and Bill had all the experience needed to design these works and prepare the specification documents. So, they were put to work, David doing the on-site works and Bill doing the main road diversion of Strangland Lane – 'Bill's Boulevard'!

However, a site survey was needed. Allotts had sent a survey team to the site led by someone who had just returned from the British Antarctic Survey. They had been at site for weeks but no survey drawings were in evidence. In desperation, David and Bill told Mr Bailey, the partner in charge of the project, that given a few days on site, they could produce the survey they needed for the design for the preliminary site works. As Mr Bailey was reluctant to agree, David and Bill offered to do this over a weekend without, of course, overtime payment, provided two nights of hotel accommodation was paid for by Allotts.

Setting off in Bill's 'banger' on Friday evening, they arrived in Ferrybridge village by the Great North Road to find they had been booked in a very run-down pub. While waiting to check in, they heard the receptionist telling a very rough-looking truck driver they were full up, however, they were expecting two young lads who were going to work at the power station and he could share a room with them. David and Bill decided this was not on and set off up the A1 to the well-appointed Brotherton Fox Inn to find rooms and checked in. "We will face the music about our expenses when we get back," they said.

Starting early on Saturday morning, by Sunday night they had completed the survey and were back at their desks in the office on Monday morning. They quickly prepared the drawings of the survey before submitting their expenses which were approved without a problem.

It was now 'hey lads hey' (work as fast as possible) to get the design drawings done with the bills of quantities and specifications so that the tender documents could be issued in time to receive the prices and appoint a contractor to start work in early September. David and Bill played a full part in this work.

The problem by July was that Mr Bailey was by then only just advertising in the *DAILY TELEGRAPH* for a resident engineer and deputy. Both should have university degrees in civil engineering with the senior man being a chartered civil engineer, and both having experience of the supervision of civil engineering works on site.

David already had the experience of being a resident engineer on works of the type to be constructed. To see that those who were to apply had to have a university degree made him 'see red', so he immediately prepared and submitted his application for the job of deputy resident engineer.

The problem Mr Bailey now had was the replies to the *DAILY TELEGRAPH* advertisement were only just coming in and work was due to start on site next week! David was called into Mr Bailey's office, "Could you be on site on Monday?"

David had his old 'banger' so could get there and said he would be on site on Monday. He used the weekend to arrange 'digs', which he found with the coal-unloading crane driver at Ferrybridge 'A' Power Station, who lived with his wife within walking distance from the site.

Work started at once with the major earthmoving. David had been resident engineer on a major earthmoving job on the Manchester Ship Canal and was in his element in charge. The contractors quickly recognised this young man knew what he was about and an appropriate relationship was established. Meanwhile, Mr Bailey was still trying to find the man to be resident civil engineer and presumably the deputy. The earthworks proceeded well with a large fleet of Caterpillar earthmovers, until one morning, the earthworks subcontractor, Paddy Merryman, came to tell David the job was done and to congratulate David that his calculations and drawings (based on that weekend survey) had resulted in an exact balance between the excavated earth and the fill, known as the 'cut and fill'.

Meanwhile, Helga, who was the one with the money, lent David £60 for a deposit for a new Austin Mini Van to replace the last of his 'bangers'. The Mini being a van was not subject to purchase tax and therefore much cheaper than a car, however, you had to drive at less than forty miles per hour.

The wedding was to be on 31st March 1962. Marriage at the end of the fiscal year was very popular as one got a full year's tax rebate being treated for tax purposes as married for the whole of the last year. The payment was £60.

There is no doubt that David's and Helga's bachelor days were spent in the company of a vibrant group of their own age who were very much 'with it' intent on having fun in the context of a wide group of friends. Now, these days were over.

Mr Bailey did not formally appoint David as deputy resident civil engineer for the construction of Ferrybridge 'C', but David, as first man on site, had possession and was not going to make it necessary to replace him!

The man chosen to be resident civil engineer, David's boss, arrived soon after David and Helga had set up home near the site and just before the contract for the main foundations was due to start.

David had several disagreements with his boss because of him overriding some of David's decisions to not accept the quality of some of the work.

During the construction of the very large reinforced concrete cooling water culverts, which would be under the turbine house, David's inspection showed major misplacement of vital water seals and advised his boss that this work should be demolished. David was overruled. This was serious and David rang Mr Bower, the engineer in charge of the project in head office, to come to site urgently to inspect the works in question. He arrived early the next morning and then called Mr Bailey who was there in no time, followed by the senior partner, Mr Atherton and the associate from the London office who had done the design for the culverts.

By mid-afternoon, Mr McAlpine, managing director of Sir Alfred McAlpine & Son, the main building contractor, had been summoned to site.

A meeting was now being held in the CEGB's site resident engineer's office to which David's boss was called, while David remained in his office. Eventually, David was called to the McAlpine site office where all the high-level 'top brass' visitors were assembled. David was informed that his boss had gone to clear his desk and would not be seen on the site again. David was asked if he thought he could take over, the CEGB resident engineer, George Leyland, having already agreed he was happy for David to do so. Of course, David said "yes". Mr Atherton turned to Mr McAlpine and said, "Now you do as David says." From then on, there was a first-class teamwork relationship between CEGB, Allotts and McAlpines and work proceeded to programme and budget.

David was now officially deputy resident civil engineer, acting resident civil engineer until his new boss was appointed. This was perhaps the most important moment of all in the whole of David's career.

CHAPTER FIVE
Starting to Change the Dreams into Reality

In 1962, young people did not expect to start married life in a house fitted out with everything. Even fifty years later, many of that generation continue to enjoy an ongoing project of ever striving to complete their dream home. Each piece of furniture bought even fifty years later being another to fill a gap in that original dream, another pleasure, each time.

David and Helga were without any capital. Helga had saved up to be able to lend David £60 before they were married to provide the deposit for the purchase of the Mini Van. She had also saved up to pay for the wedding. David, for his part, had made a good start to his career and could look forward to an above average income for a civil engineer of his generation.

Having started work at Ferrybridge in the autumn of 1961, and being engaged to marry Helga in March 1962, David needed to find them a home to come to after the wedding. They dreamed of living in the country. It would need to be near Ferrybridge. That meant "go east, young man!" So, off he went on foot due east into rural Yorkshire. There was a lane on the map leading due east from the A1 at the Brotherton Fox Inn. After a walk of about two miles, he came to the very small village, a hamlet really, of Birkin. In the country, if you want to know something, you knock on a door and ask. What better than to ask a farmer, they always like 'a crack' (a chat)! So, he knocked on the Poskit's farm house door.

Having explained why he was there and that he was working at the new power station site, he must have seemed like a 'good country lad', as Mr Poskit took him passed the next field and showed him a bungalow which he offered to rent for £3 per week, which included a special drainage rate levied in the floodplain of that part of Yorkshire. It was perfect. "Not a bad day's house hunting!" David thought. Helga could move back to her beloved Yorkshire into a practically new bungalow. David went to bring her from Cheshire and the deal was sealed. Helga could now start planning her new home. David moved in with a colleague from site to share the house until the wedding.

Helga was now busy planning the wedding. Neither she nor David wanted other than a simple wedding. It was, to them, about committing themselves to a life together, not an excuse for a big party. The guest list was closest family members, Helga's mother and father, David's mother now divorced from his father, both David's sister Judith and Helga's sister Alison, the maid of honour, and her husband David, Helga's aunt Nora Stockton and her uncle Arthur Stockton, David's uncle Sandy and best man, Jim Kent, and his wife, Gill, David's granny and her old friend and Helga's godmother, Hilda Brighouse, as well as Helga's parents' old friend, Mrs Smith. Unfortunately, Alison's husband, David, was away at sea on the day of the wedding. Although David's father and new wife Pat were invited, they turned down the invitation. A traditional Church of England wedding was held at St Anne's Church in Sale followed by a reception at the Roebuck Inn in Mobberley, a few miles away in the Cheshire countryside. It turned out to also be a rather special day for the two oldest guests, one from each of the two family guest lists, with David's granny meeting Helga's godmother again after so very many years. The two were old friends from the time when Hilda Brighouse used to be a regular guest at The Scafell Hotel in Rosthwaite in Cumberland when David's granny and grandfather were the proprietors.

28. David and Helga's small family wedding

There was snow in the air that day, as the happy couple set off in their Mini Van for a very short honeymoon in Cornwall, stopping for the first night at the Royal Hotel in Ross-on-Wye. On the way back, they stayed a couple of nights with Jim and Gill in Buckinghamshire, they vacating their double bed for the honeymooners! Jim and Gill had only been married a few weeks before!

The essentials of furnishings were assembled to add to the few provided in the rented bungalow called Ashdene. Granny provided some sitting room chairs and silver items, which included a rather splendid solid silver corinthian column table lamp. David and Helga had bought a second-hand dressing table and old kitchen chairs each costing seven shillings and sixpence. Over the months leading up to the wedding Kellogg's had run a promotion for silver-plated canteen cutlery. By collecting the vouchers from breakfast cereal packets from all their friends and even colleagues on the power station site, a full canteen of cutlery, even including fish knives and forks, was available by the start of David and Helga's married life. The quality was such that they were in constant use for about forty years!

Returning from honeymoon via Sale to load their now worldly goods into their Mini Van, our honeymooners drove over the snow-packed Pennines to arrive at Ashdene in Birkin ten days after the wedding.

On the following Monday David set off to work leaving Helga marooned in the tiny hamlet of Birkin served with no public transport and only a minute village shop, not even a pub. However they had bought some meat. Helga says she knew how to cook the meat, but how do you make gravy? Nevertheless she had two cookbooks, her engagement present from David, *GOOD HOUSEKEEPING'S PICTURE RECIPES*, and *THROUGH YORKSHIRE'S KITCHEN DOOR – RECIPE BOOK* compiled from recipes submitted by members of the Yorkshire Federation of Women's Institutes. The Internet where you can look anything up, was fifty years into the future! Both books were still in use those fifty years later, although by then Helga's cookbook library had expanded to shelves of books and filed cuttings covering every kind of cooking.

Helga had not passed her driving test so David's sister lent her a bicycle which enabled her to ride to the nearest bus route passing through Beal some three miles from Birkin. From here the bus ran to Pontefract, the nearest small market town.

Well the dream had started to become reality, it was not like being in heaven, however at least it was not a nightmare!

David had a well-defined professional life to occupy him supervising the construction at Ferrybridge. Helga was now a housewife, a completely new lifestyle to the city worker she had been in Manchester. However, she was not fazed by her new role and from not knowing how to make gravy, she soon had matters in relating to running the home under control on a budget of just over £3 per week. Weekly shopping was in Pontefract with small essentials such as sugar, tea and matches available in the tiny village shop. Soon, a 'saviour' called. It was Mr Scoley, the butcher from Monk Fryston, in his travelling shop. Not only did he sell Helga the meat she needed but he taught her about the cuts. As the months passed by with one or two dramas taking place on the site at Ferrybridge where David was still in charge, Helga embarked on her life of helping others, supporting older members of the family, in time, becoming a mother and developing a very active involvement in many charities.

Miss Dixon, the lady who owned the village shop became ill with cancer. In those days, there were practically no cures for cancer, indeed, it was never referred to, it being a taboo subject. Helga volunteered to help in the shop, unpaid, taking over the day to day running as Miss Dixon's health deteriorated. Helga continued with this until David and Helga moved back to Sale. Miss Dixon died soon after. David and Helga also started to invite friends and family to stay. Jim and Gill Kent, Bill Hoskinson and wife, little niece Sally Anne (running excited up to the house exclaiming, "I am on my holidays") all came. David's Granny Badrock also came to stay.

Unfortunately, she had a fall resulting in a stay of several weeks in hospital in Pontefract, Helga being a regular visitor, taking the extra bits needed to make life better for Granny. Eventually, she returned to Cheshire by ambulance, not being fit enough to get into the Mini Van.

The social life was centred on the professional and management staff engaged in building Ferrybridge 'C' Power Station. It was quite an active social life with a good deal of eating out, usually at the contractors' expense, an accepted practice in those days. However, David and Helga reciprocated by having gatherings at Ashdene, particularly after the Christmas period, when again as was the practice, contractors gave small gifts to their clients and the consultants, such as a bottle of spirits and a large pack of cigarettes, even a Christmas turkey. Since there were by now quite a few contractors on site, these gifts became quite a hoard. David was anxious not to be influenced by these gifts so Helga would arrange parties at Ashdene so that those involved in the giving were also involved in the consumption.

The garden provided a new task for Helga with some support from David. Helga cut the lawn with a rather old push mower, no doubt, needing sharpening. One evening, David came home to be greeted by Helga with a very big smile on her face. To mark the end of the earthmoving, Paddy Merryman, the earthmoving contactor, had arrived with a motor mower for David and Helga. "That must go back at once," said David. And it did that evening. David had observed the high professional ethics of his father and put these into practice throughout his career. Helga was not best pleased to see the mower being loaded into the Mini Van!

Uncle Sandy came for each Christmas and after the first Christmas, they joined him on holiday in Zermatt. Not the cheapest of places. However, quite unexpectedly, David received a bonus of £50 in recognition of the extra responsibility he had taken on after the original resident civil engineer had been sacked. This was a significant sum and went quite some way to the cost of the holiday. They flew from Gatwick, David sitting in fear, without saying a word throughout the flight. This was a man who, in due course, was to spend more time in the air in some years than an intercontinental KLM captain he met.

The period while David was acting resident civil engineer was not without incidents or critical moments for the right decision. All works to be covered up in concrete were inspected and approved by David's site staff, now including graduate engineers, clerks of works and inspectors. Nevertheless, no written records were kept of this procedure, with it being up to the section staff to ensure the procedure was followed. There was a fully equipped materials testing laboratory on site being part of the resident civil engineer's establishment. Sample concrete test cubes were taken from all important pours of concrete and tested for strength at seven and twenty-eight days. David, himself, would carry out the inspections of the foundation material to make sure it was as expected to be to carry the huge weights of the power station buildings and structures. He had, in fact, prepared the site investigation contract for the borehole and soils and rock testing and therefore well understood the ground conditions needed.

The two chimneys at Ferrybridge were to be seven hundred and fifty feet tall and would be the tallest in Europe, if not in the world. (They did make an entry in the *GUINNESS BOOK OF RECORDS*). They were to be constructed on massive reinforced concrete pad foundations sitting on the limestone. The site investigation had established that this rock formation had a soft weathered top surface.

Where the main buildings were to be sited, the rock was near the surface so that large mass concrete foundations could be adopted having excavated through the weathered layer. However, it was known that the rock shelved away quickly between the main building area and the cooling towers area.

Once the excavation for the first chimney foundation had been completed, David was informed so he could decide that the exposed rock was as expected and could take the weight of the chimney. Using the simple tools of a steel reinforcing rod and a sledgehammer, he arranged for the rod to be driven into the rock while he observed. It kept going down a few feet. A scaffold platform was constructed to enable a much longer rod to be driven into the rock. It kept going! The long and the short of it is that work was stopped so that a completely different design of foundation on piling could be prepared. This is just an example of the responsibility of those on site have beyond just following the design drawings and specification.

Another incident of note involved the wrong positioning of a block of reinforced concrete cooling water culvert about ten feet by ten feet and twenty-five feet long. A big piece of concrete! The remedy was dynamite and start again!

After several months of David in charge, Allotts finally appointed the new resident civil engineer. This time they got it right. Colonel Cartwright-Taylor had just retired as commanding officer of the Royal Engineers, that is to say, the chief engineer for the British

29. *David getting down to "the works"*

Army. He brought major project management experience. Above all, he introduced quality assurance procedure records that were well ahead of practice at that time. Every inspection was signed by the contractor's section engineer or foreman and, after approval, was signed off by the Allott staff member supervising that area of work. These records, together with the laboratory test results, were kept on file should they be needed for reference in the future. This standard set at Ferrybridge would be followed and become a norm throughout the construction industry. Site safety was also a top priority, even the wearing of safety helmets was new for construction sites, all professional, management and supervisory staff being required to wear them. With this example, in time, all men on site accepted the practice.

David now continued to look after the civil engineering and other structures under construction, including the chimneys, cooling towers and coal unloading facilities for rail and river deliveries. Meanwhile, the main building steelwork erection and finishes had got underway.

Most of the construction for the Unit 1 of the four-unit 2000 MW power station had taken place when David was recalled to take up a design office role in head office in Sale in late 1964. Helga had passed her driving test and they now had a Triumph Spitfire sports car.

At the minimum age allowed, David had submitted his papers and design (for the lower leading jetty at Latchford Locks on the Manchester Ship Canal) for his professional interview to become a fully qualified chartered engineer. The interviewers having started the interview by suggesting next time the layout of his career report could be improved, proceeded to question him on the design of a small effluent treatment plant he had done as a fill-in job just after he joined Allotts. The impression given was that neither of them knew anything about port engineering or power stations. So, proceeding to the essay room after lunch, not knowing what subject he would have to write about, he was feeling he had not been given the chance to demonstrate in the interview the broad experience and level of responsibility he had had in his career to date. However, he was asked to produce a paper on the quality control of concrete construction. Never mind a paper on the subject; he could have written a book on the subject! He passed, but being only twenty-four, he had to wait until his twenty-fifth birthday before he could refer to himself as a chartered engineer and use the letters of his chartered qualification, AMICE, after his name.

While in Yorkshire, David had played rugby for Selby Old Boys. However, he decided to retire after a tough match against a side at Easter which included strapping school leavers of eighteen who had given a hard time!

With the move back to head office in Sale, David and Helga needed to find a new home. They used the approach that had worked out well in finding Ashdene. They wanted to live in the country in Cheshire and set off to spend a weekend with Helga's parents in Sale to go house hunting. They came across a derelict cottage in Aston-by-Budworth between Sale and Northwich. It was down a quiet lane which led to a wood next to the cottage. It was difficult to explore round the cottage as the garden was so overgrown. They did not have the money to offer to buy it, but might they be able to rent it and make it habitable? First, who owned it? Well, who better to ask than the nearby farmer? "It belongs to the estate," Mr Acton, the farmer, explained. "Whose estate?" asked David.

"Lord Ashbrook of Arley Hall nearby," the farmer replied. "And who are the land agents looking after the Arley Estate?" David asked.

"Mellor Speakman and Hall of Manchester," came the answer.

Once again, a good crack with a farmer was producing some vital information. So, on Monday morning David rang Mellor Speakman and Hall to see if the cottage might be for rent. Only getting as far as a junior staff member, he was told the Ashbrooks intended to renovate the cottage and would then offer it for rent. David and Helga then thought who did they know who might know Lord Ashbrook. They knew Geoff Rylands well who was a close friend of Uncle Sandy. Geoff was chairman of Rylands Wire Ltd, a very large manufacturer based in Warrington.

"Geoff, do you know Lord Ashbrook?" asked David.

"Yes, I know the Ashbrooks well and in fact, Lady Ashbrook serves on the magistrates' bench with me in Warrington."

David explained that they wanted to rent the cottage, known as Stonegate Cottage. They were prepared to do the renovations. Within a day, David received a call, this time from the senior partner of Mellor, Speakman and Hall, Mr Hall himself. He had heard that they might make good tenants for Stonegate Cottage and could they come to see him. A meeting was arranged. No, they could not rent Stonegate Cottage just yet, but they could as soon as it had been renovated.

"But what will you do until then?" Mr Hall asked. "Lady Ashbrook has offered you a flat in Arley Hall which she says will be rent free on the condition you do not interfere with the renovation work at Stonegate Cottage." Looking back, this seems to have been too good to be true. Nevertheless, David and Helga moved into Barracks Flat in Arley Hall until Stonegate Cottage was available to rent at £6 per week. Geoff must have given some one hell of a good reference! They bought Stonegate Cottage eleven years later for £13,000.

So, it was in 1964 that David took up his new role in head office in charge of the design and preparation of specifications for all work except the main buildings for the now planned new 2000 MW coal-fired power station at Didcot in Berkshire. Although he originally wanted to be a civil engineer, but not working on power stations, now he had a deep knowledge of the subject and from now on, this would be the main focus for the rest of his career. Indeed, he found himself now working for one of the two leading power station civil consulting engineers in the UK, a company which was to become involved in such projects throughout the world. Nor would he ever in the future find he had a university graduated engineer of his generation as his senior. His career was launched.

CHAPTER SIX
Catastrophic Failure
However, Human Tragedy Avoided – Just!

On 28th December 1879, at the height of a storm of wind and rain, the first Tay Bridge collapsed just as a train was crossing and every one of the eighty passengers on the train was drowned.

30. Tay Bridge collapse

On 1st November 1965, at Ferrybridge 'C' Power Station, three of the largest natural draft cooling towers in the world collapsed at

*31. Ferrybridge Cooling
Tower collapsing*

intervals during gale-force winds. The towers were structurally complete, though not in operation. The construction supervision had been part of David's responsibility while working as deputy resident civil engineer. The first tower collapsed at ten ten a.m., the second at ten thirty a.m. and the third at eleven fifity a.m.

David was working in his office in the Allott & Lomax headquarters in Sale when the news spread through the building of the dramatic events unfolding at Ferrybridge.

The call came from Arnold Atherton, the senior partner, "David, could you come up to my office." David remembers vividly the start of the conversation. "Have you heard what has happened at Ferrybridge?"

"Yes, Mr Atherton, there has been a collapse of cooling towers."

"What do you think about that?"

David gave an immediate and confident reply, "I can assure you that the towers were fully inspected at every stage throughout construction with the materials for the concrete and the concrete itself being tested. The full record of the inspection and testing is held in our site office and the towers will be shown to have been built to specification and the drawings, with some very small out of tolerance in the overall line of the shell, it being impossible to keep to the specified tolerance as the heat of sunshine actually moves the concrete more than the tolerance specified." David went on to explain the thorough inspection procedures of raw materials, sand and gravel testing as well as checking of cement quality, the checking to make sure reinforcement was properly in place before concreting and then concrete samples being tested in the site laboratory for strength at seven and twenty-eight days. "I am sure the failure is not due to the quality of construction," David said. Indeed, in spite of the quite dramatic event, David was really convinced that the workmanship was up to standard and that the quality assurance records would show this to be the case.

These records together with the surveys of the collapse sites were an immediate focus of the investigation into the reason for the failure and supported what David had been able to tell Mr Atherton on the morning of the incident. The investigation was then able to fully turn its attention to the design criteria and the design mathematics. However, while the news of one tower after another collapsing came through, no news of any injury or deaths at the site came through. Fortunately, there had been no such serious incidents. But human tragedy which would have set the Ferrybridge failure alongside the Tay Bridge disaster in the history of engineering had only just been avoided.

The towers were being constructed by Kier under one of the many main civil contracts on the site being supervised by Allotts. While the rest of the civil engineering was being designed by Allotts, the concrete cooling towers were a design and build contract to the design of the Kier subsidiary company, Film Cooling Towers Ltd. Allotts were therefore not the designers, nor responsible for the design criteria.

At the time of the incident, Kiers were running their site compliment down prior for final inspection by Allotts and handover to CEGB. By this time, the Kier staff on site was only the general foreman, a junior engineer, a secretary, a wages clerk, a store man and forty-five men.

Earlier in the morning, the forty-five men were sweeping up in the first tower which was to collapse.

There had been considerable discussion in the Kier site office as to whether it was thought safe for the men to keep working. At ten a.m., just ten minutes before the first tower collapsed, it was decided to blow the whistle to stop work and send the men home. So, by just those ten minutes, a human tragedy on the scale of the Tay Bridge disaster was avoided.

However, in engineering terms, it was just as big an issue. There had been a major design failure, the reason for which was not understood. Furthermore, it had occurred on a very important public utility site where the first of several power stations was being built to meet the rapidly increasing demand for electricity, at 7% per annum, which would double the amount of electricity which would be needed in ten years.

Matters were raised in the House of Lords on 16th November. "My Lords," began the Earl of Bessborough, "I beg to ask the Question which stands in my name on the Order Paper." To ask Her Majesty's Government whether they will make a statement regarding the concrete cooling towers which were blown over at the Ferrybridge 'C'

32. Ferrybridge Cooling Towers collapsed

Power Station near Knottingley, Yorkshire, during the recent gales; whether models of the towers were properly tested in wind tunnels and what steps are being taken to prevent similar occurrences in the future."

Lord Stonham, the Joint Parliamentary Secretary of State, Home Office replied. Describing the incident, he went on to say while towers approaching the size of those at Ferrybridge had been tested and had operated for several years without mishap, there was to be a committee of inquiry to investigate the cause of the Ferrybridge collapse.

The Earl of Bessborough raised a number of possible causes of the collapse, and then asked, "Is the result of this going to be further cuts in electricity this winter, or some restrictions?"

The debate continued without getting anywhere with reference to other towers and even whether they were Labour or Tory towers!

Back to reality! It was now of the utmost importance that the reason for the failure was established. Was it due to poor workmanship or was the design at fault?

The cooling towers were three hundred and seventy-five feet high and two hundred and ninety feet diameter at the base. The thin shell walls were only five inches thick. In contrast, the shell of an egg as large as a Ferrybridge tower would be twenty-five inches thick.

The CEGB investigation reported that, "When records and inspection of the collapse structures revealed no significant deficiencies in construction and materials, the committee turned to the review of the design of the towers."

The most significant impact of the design failure was the resultant theoretical advances in the field of structural dynamics. The entire approach to the design was reassessed and the results were ultimately incorporated into international structural design methods and building codes.

CHAPTER SEVEN
Nine to Five and Two Becomes Three

Although the Second World War, like the First, had impacted on the structure of society, the class structure was still very much in evidence. The middle class could no longer afford live-in staff, although David's mother had a live-in maid until his sister Judith went away to boarding school. The higher echelons of the class structure, the upper class, were those of 'old money'. This being evident in the leadership of the country with prime ministers, Sir Harold Macmillan and Sir Alex Douglas-Home, and Sir Winston Churchill before them, all from wealthy landed families. Those in 'the professions' regarded themselves in the upper middle class, thinking themselves as above those 'in trade', that is to say, those who owned small and medium-sized businesses. Those in the lower class were, with justification, looking to improve their lot and 'flexing their muscles' with leadership from the trade unions. Stanley Matthews, the leading footballer of the day, indeed regarded as one of the best ever, was paid about £15 a week. Put in context, an average nice suburban house cost £2,000.

In summary, you could say those at the top already had money, those in the professions placed strong ethics and provision of service before financial reward, while those 'in trade' looked to the opportunity to make their fortunes in an ever-improving economy. Film stars did make fortunes.

Consequently, the professions were held in high regard, the

family doctor being the pinnacle of local society. Chartered engineers as consulting engineers were engaged to design, specify and draw up the construction programme, issue tenders, recommend the contractors, supervise the works on site, certify payments to the contractors and finally give the completion certificates at the end of construction. The merit of this approach, involving the contractors being paid against a priced bill of quantities, was that at the outset, the contactors were not required to tender a final fixed price for the work, that is 'a turnkey price' for the job. Its shortcoming was that it was incumbent on the consulting engineers to produce an accurate estimate at the outset on which the client could base his financial plan. At that time, there was major investment in the nation's infrastructure, roads, sewage treatment and power stations. These works were undertaken in the main with this approach.

Likewise, the other professions with their strong ethics were righty trusted by society. Teachers ran the schools, bankers ran the banks, lawyers did not engage in advertising at all, never mind grubbing around for business on a 'no win - no fee basis'. There was no need for 'Government watchdog' departments. Even the major transactions in the stock exchange were agreed with a shake of hands and members did not renege on deals; their 'word was their bond.'

It was against this background that David had entered his profession. And it was these principles and ethics he applied throughout his career. Helga for her part, like most other middle-class wives of professional men of her generation, saw her task of building up the home, looking after their family and supporting her husband in his career when she could. She was to play this role to the full, supporting older members of the family as well as 'keeping the home fires burning' and, in time, making a key contribution to the development of Allotts' business, by then very international. Helga's age group was to be the last to adopt such a role which was to be dismissed by those ten years younger when going out to work became the norm.

Now, after several months living rent free in Barracks Flat in Arley Hall, the move to Stonegate Cottage in Aston by Budworth took place in early 1965. The savings from having no rent while in the flat were used to buy the carpets for the cottage.

Although Helga was now pregnant, she did most of the decorating inside the cottage, which had been left unpainted after the renovations. With three bedrooms, a kitchen, living/dining room and a downstairs bathroom/WC, Stonegate Cottage made an ideal home in which to start a family. Outside the garden was a wilderness although there was evidence of their having been an orchard with a damson tree and a cooking apple tree. Needless to say, just as at Birkin, there was no public transport serving Aston by Budworth. Well, these two always wanted to live in the country!

Helga set about the task of creating a comfortable home and indeed the garden, while by June becoming a mum. Both she and David wanted their child born at home. For a first child, this was by now not the norm. Nevertheless, the doctor accepted their wish and James was born on 4th June 1965, with a midwife in attendance and David sitting downstairs waiting for news from the bedroom upstairs. Fathers did not attend births in those days. It was not an easy birth but in the end, all was well. Shortly after the birth, the first visitor was the old farmer, Mr Acton, from just down the road. It was he who had explained to Helga and David who owned Stonegate Cottage.

For the next two and a half years until early 1967, David had a relatively routine working life based in the Allott head office in Sale, half an hour's drive away. Helga says there was no evidence of David having a nine to five routine! Helga needed the car twice a week and would drive David to and from work on those days.

Nearest neighbours were the Furness farming family, Ken and Sue. They became lifelong friends and Helga became 'Auntie' Helga to their children, David, Libby, Richard and Anthony. She would go with Sue and the children, including James, for caravan holidays each year in Anglesey, for Ken as a farmer had no time for holidays!

David was leading the design team for the civil engineering work for Didcot Power Station. While these were major works, they were normal jobs for David and his experienced staff, many of whom had worked on Ferrybridge. The exception was the design which had to be developed for the cooling water culverts. The CEGB wanted these to be a piped system rather than the Allott 'standard' concrete culverts. Allotts was proud of their designs on both Ferrybridge and its sister station at Radcliffe near Nottingham which had proved to cost less per megawatt installed for the buildings and civil engineering than those designed by their competitors. On the face of it, a piped system for the cooling water would be more expensive than concrete. David developed a design with one twelve-foot diameter steel pipe instead of two pipes, the concrete culvert system at Ferrybridge and Radcliffe being based on twin culverts. The twelve-feet diameter pipes needed to be buried in the ground with just earth surround to be economical. The Armco Company of America had developed a corrugated steel pipe system with just earth surround to form highway culverts and bridges. David figured a smooth pipe structure could behave the same way. Working with Professor Schofield of UMIST and later Cambridge, the system was adopted and research put in hand to determine the theory behind this empirically proven type of structure, while David consulted American engineers, who at that time were developing the same approach for long-distance irrigation pipelines.

*33. 12 foot diameter steel cooling water pipe installation,
Didcot Power Station*

By this time, Lin Ollier, who had been the partner in charge of the London office returned to the head office in Sale. David was given the additional job of leading a site selection study for the CEGB's next nuclear power station, reporting to Lin Ollier who was to prove to be David's third mentor in his career, the others having been Mr Hardy at the Manchester Ship Canal and Mr Atherton, senior partner at Allotts. The study involved investigating a very large number of possible locations east of Birmingham. It was the most expensive site feasibility study to find a power station site the CEGB had ever commissioned. All the sites were underlain with keuper marl, a material which could be soft and weathered to rocklike. The resultant soil/rock mechanics site and laboratory testing led David to the conclusion that none of the sites was suitable to carry the very heavy loads of nuclear reactors. Mr Ollier must have decided it would be valuable experience for David to go to London to the CEGB headquarters to report this to the chief planning engineer, Mr Reg Hunt. Going in fear and dread of what the reaction would be to such a negative recommendation after such an expensive study, David was relieved when Mr Hunt said, "This is very good advice David. Our nuclear reactors at Oldbury are on marl and are sinking at present and causing concern." The study then turned to focus on Heysham on Morecambe Bay, also a complicated site with a geological fault. However, with thorough investigation, the site was found to be suitable on one side of the fault. In due course two nuclear power stations were built on the same side of the fault.

It was coming up to the time when Mr Atherton would retire. David was conscious of the support, encouragement and opportunity he had given him. Soon, Lin Ollier was to take over as senior partner. During Mr Atherton's time as senior partner, the company had grown from a small office in Barton Arcade in Manchester to having a London design office and its new eight-storey headquarters office which had been purpose designed by the company. This had been achieved against a background of securing contracts one after another for the design of power stations, including three of the largest in the world. Before standing down, he saw the opportunity to strengthen the senior staff and brought Roger Hyde into the company as an associate (the most senior position outside the partners).

Roger was a chartered civil engineer and a graduate of Cambridge University. He had just been responsible for the design of the prestressed concrete pressure vessels for the nuclear reactors at Olbury nuclear power station. Like David, he had been to public school and socially they were at ease with each other. However, their approach to engineering differed and would cause some tension between them. Roger was a brilliant mathematician; he would need to be to have designed the nuclear reactor pressure vessels. By now, David saw his approach to engineering as providing leadership based on the vision he had of the engineering concept which would be developed in its detail by his staff. Roger seemed to approach the subject mathematically.

Roger took over responsibility for the Didcot project reporting to the partner in charge. The design was very well advanced with construction under way. David's role on the project was to some extent reduced in so far as he now lost the duty of attending the regular site meetings. Roger was clearly not happy with the twelve-foot diameter flexible steel cooling water pipe system based on empirical methods with the theory of how it worked only just being researched by Professor Schofield. To Roger, the idea that the structural behaviour of the pipe under load could not be determined mathematically must have been a horror! However, there was no turning back, the pipes were being installed. In addition to the laboratory testing of small scale models of the pipes at UMIST, strain gauge tests were to be conducted on the full-scale pipes as they were being installed. This latter exercise did not receive the attention it should have had, much to David's displeasure. The research had to proceed without what would have been valuable additional data from site. The soundness of the concept was finally well and truly tested when the first of the boiler drums weighing a few thousand tons was rolled over the pipe system followed by three more boiler drums over the coming months. A technical publication, *DESIGN AND CONSTRUCTION OF BURIED THIN-WALL PIPES* was released, although Professor Schofield's theory was the subject of some dispute within engineering circles involved with water projects.

Nevertheless, the concept worked!

Perhaps the partners were aware of the professional tensions between Roger and David. David was given new duties in addition to those he had on Didcot, but now reporting directly to Lin Ollier. In early 1967, it was announced that C. S. Allott & Son, working with the renowned mechanical and electrical consulting engineers, Kennedy and Donkin, had been appointed by the Comisión Federal de Electricidad of Mexico for the design of two 300-MW power stations, one an extension of the existing Valle de México Power Plant near Mexico City, the other some hundred miles to the north at Salamanca. Lin Ollier was to be the partner in charge and David would report to him as the project engineer responsible for managing all the Allott work on the project, including interfacing with the client in Mexico.

While all this had been going on, David had become a director of the family business in the Lake District, Scafell Hotel in Rosthwaite, run by his Uncle Sandy. The hotel had been inundated by a major flood which resulted in its closure. David, as a non-executive unpaid director, took on the task of preparing the scheme to renovate the hotel with extra rooms, all en suite and updated kitchen.

Meanwhile, Helga was developing a beautiful cottage garden from the wilderness that had surrounded Stonegate Cottage when they moved in. James was becoming a little boy.

Work started in the office on the Mexican project on 27th February 1967. On 7th March, Lin Ollier and David set off from Manchester Airport on the daily BOAC VC10 flight to New York with an onward connection to Mexico City. Helga and James saw David board the aircraft from the outside viewing platform above the departure gate. Security was limited in those days, even the first airliner highjack had not taken place. Any semblance of a 'nine to five' routine for David was over, forever.

CHAPTER EIGHT
Allotts – The World's Second Longest Established Consulting Engineers

David, having been inspired by reading L.T.C. Rolt's biographies of the great engineers of the Industrial Revolution and the Victorian era, Telford road and canal builder, George and Robert Stephenson together with Brunel, the railway builders, now found the company he was working for, C. S. Allott & Son, had a direct link to the Stephensons.

Charles Sneath Allott was born in 1842. At the age of fourteen, he left the famous Lincoln City School to become articled (under an agreed training period) to a civil engineer, Lewis Henry Moorson and served his pupilage on the construction of the Ringwood to Christchurch Railway. At the age of twenty-one, he joined William (later Sir William) Fairbairn's Engineering Company in Manchester. There he remained to become the assistant manager, deputy to

32. Charles Sneath Allott

Sir William and then to his son, Thomas. When Sir William died in 1874, the company was wound up.

Sir William was a contemporary of George and Robert Stephenson and was involved with them on railway projects. Fairbairn specialised in structural engineering being in the forefront of bridge

35. Floating out of Fairbairn's box girder during construction of the Britannia Bridge Menai

design and fabrication. In particular, he developed the box- shaped tubular girder concept.

This system was adopted for his designs of the bridge at Conwy and the Menai Britannia Bridge between the Wales mainland and Anglesey for the Stephenson Chester to Holyhead Railway. While working for the Fairbairn Engineering Company, Allott was responsible for bridges on the Intercontinental Railway in Canada as well as the roofs of Liverpool Street Station in London and the Royal Albert Hall. The latter was particularly challenging as it was required to support a round dome. The finished structure was fully

assembled in the Manchester works and tested, before being dismantled and finally erected in London.

When the scaffold supports that had been in place to support the roof as it was assembled were removed, the roof

36. Test assembly of Royal Albert Hall Roof

was hailed as 'a great engineering triumph' and the good news was relayed to the Prince of Wales and Prime Minister, Gladstone. Those were the days when there was the well-known saying, "What Manchester does today, the rest of the world does tomorrow."

Such was the status of Sir William and engineers of that day that as many as 70,000 people were estimated to have lined the streets of Manchester as his funeral cortege passed.

Lady Fairbairn found herself with the archives of her husband's company. The story goes that she turned to Charles Allott and asked if they would be of interest to him. They included many of the original drawings of numerous railway bridges of which copies would have been extremely limited, there being no way to reproduce these except by hand drawing the copy. Allott accepted the gift of the drawings and found himself in a strong position to establish a client base with the railway companies when he established his own consulting engineering practise in 1875 in Chapel Walk in Manchester.

Early work involved more railway bridges followed by two cotton mills for Brazil and China, which not only involved the design, but the management of shipping out all the equipment and even the paving slabs for the floors and then construction of the mills. In 1890, his son Henry (Harry) Newmark Allott joined the firm, being taken into partnership in 1898, the company then becoming known as C. S. Allott & Son. Harry had studied at the Manchester Technical School and been articled to Mr William Hunt, chief engineer of the Lancaster and Yorkshire Railway.

The first power station the company became responsible for, as civil consulting engineers to Manchester Corporation, was Stuart Street Manchester at the turn of the century. Charles Allott died suddenly in February 1907. Harry took over as senior partner and more power station work followed at Agecroft and Barton, also in

Manchester. Other work of note involved working with the mechanical and electrical consulting engineers, Kennedy & Donkin (K&D) on the electrification of Southern Railways, which included Wimbledon Power Station. C. S. Allott & Son were also the civil and structural engineers for the London Underground Lots Road Power Station

With the move of the chief engineer of the Manchester Corporation to the London Power Company, C. S. Allott & Son were appointed civil consultants for the proposed Battersea Power Station. Sadly, Henry (Harry) Allott died suddenly on 17th June 1929 soon after the appointment. The issue facing the London Power Company was: without the leadership of Harry Allott were C. S. Allott & Son equipped and sufficiently skilled enough to handle the task for Battersea.

Arthur Creswell Dean, a nephew by marriage to Harry Allott, had joined the partnership in 1926 and was now senior partner after only three years as a partner. He had been the resident engineer on Wimbledon Power Station. He faced an intensive interview with the top management of the London Power Company and was successful in persuading them to keep the commission with C. S. Allott & Son.

Sir Giles Gilbert Scott is often referred to as the architect of Battersea Power Station. In fact, as reported in *THE MANCHESTER GUARDIAN* of 14th February 1934, the building design was originated and the architecture developed by A. C. Dean, as senior partner of C. S. Allott & Son, with collaboration from Manchester architects, Halliday & Agate. The interior art deco was by Halliday & Agate.

C. S. Allott & Son developed the building design through several stages, taking account of the design developments of the mechanical plant and associated systems, particularly in relation to flue gas cleaning. The familiar configuration of the building, originally as phase one with two chimneys, had been established by C. S. Allott & Son and construction started, when Sir Giles Gilbert Scott was called in at that late stage as consultant architect. The final stage of A. C. Dean's design was produced with Sir Giles's assistance. The reinforced concrete design for the chimneys was by L. G. Mouchel, the inventor and pioneer of reinforced concrete.

When completed, the appearance of the power station was well received by the public.

37. Battersea Power Station

With their involvement at Wimbledon, Lots Road and Battersea, Allotts had provided the civil and structural engineering for the power stations that provided most of the electricity for London.

Allotts had a difficult time during the recession in the 1930s, there being a story that Mr Dean kept the business going with financial support from his wife's dancing school!

Work picked up as the War approached. After the War, C. S. Allott & Son was involved at the outset of the construction of the world's first nuclear power station at Calder Hall in Cumberland, being involved in the civil engineering with Lin Ollier (later to become chairman of the Allotts), being one of the first men on site when construction started in the spring of 1953. The company went on to be involved in a series of power station projects with Arnold Atherton taking over as senior partner a few years after returning from War service. Before then, there had been an involvement in over twenty power stations, including some overseas.

When C. S. Allott & Son moved into their new eight-storey office block headquarters in Sale in 1967, one could see seven 'Allott' power stations from the roof. During the years that followed, the company was engaged as the civil/structural consultants on a further twenty power stations located across the world from Argentina to Hong Kong.

Allotts and their much-respected rivals, L. G. Mouchel & Partners, had become to the era of thermal power station construction what the Stephensons and Brunel had been to the era of railway construction.

CHAPTER NINE
A Balancing Act while "The Times They Are A Changin'"

From the day David flew off to Mexico in 1979, David and Helga were facing a new and complex life pattern. It was to have its good and bad features. Helga would spend time at home with David away. Until James went away to boarding school some five and a half years later, he was there for company. The plus was that in the years ahead, Helga would travel from time to time on David's business trips and saw much of the world.

Helga's task was to 'keep the home fires burning'. She created and ran an excellent home while also making a beautiful cottage garden. She even mowed and kept the lawns in good shape!

She had been able to read since she was four. Now, she could find time to improve her education. As a member of a book club, she bought books on British history, horticulture, gardening and ceramics. She read them all. With her excellent memory, she could carry this knowledge with her in the years ahead to the point that she could hold her own in conversations with those who had had the advantage of studying these subjects at university. Her library became a feature of the home she created.

Nevertheless, it was vital that David and Helga had common interests to share and enjoy when David was at home. His business trips were generally for less than a month, often just a week or so. But the frequency was such that a KLM intercontinental airline captain he met said David spent more time away from home than he did. In one year, David spent just over half of the nights away from home.

For a few years, holidays were spent in North Yorkshire on the farms where Helga had spent her early childhood and where her parents now lived in a house rented from the Cross family and in the Lake District staying with Uncle Sandy in Borrowdale, in this case going back to where David had grown up as a small child.

From the mid 1960s, the UK entered a period of economic decline and social unrest. Race riots led to the Race Relations Act being passed in 1965, outlawing discrimination on grounds of colour, race, ethnic or national origins in a public place. However, to do so was a civil not a criminal offence. The clashes had been in areas where those from Commonwealth countries were living, having come to the UK after the War. Religion was not the issue. Many of those from the Caribbean took vital jobs on the London Underground and other railways while those from the Indian subcontinent tended to take jobs in the textile industry.

With hindsight, the advent of the Race Relations Act can be seen as the beginning of the end of free speech in the UK. Prior to that, one could speak in public at Speakers Corner in Hyde Park in London on any subject providing the police did not consider violence was being provoked. In 1967, race relations law was strengthened to make race discrimination a criminal offence. In the years that followed, those of minority ethnic background when claiming to be offended, turned to the law to bring action against those expressing a view contrary to their own, especially on issues relating to religion. Increasingly, causing any offence became more and more an issue in society, even the old jokes about 'the Englishman, the Irishman, the Scotsman and the Welshman' could lead to interpretation as racialist. Consequently, the great majority of the population became inhibited about raising issues relating to religion and the impact of the changes brought about by a multicultural society with its impact on the fundamentals of British values which were being compromised. At the time of writing in 2015, 'political correctness' in UK universities had become so outrageous, indeed farcical, that free expression was being inhibited to the extent that there was campus censorship of anything that caused the least offence. Consequently there was reaction to those wishing to debate controversial subjects, leading to what became known as 'Safe Space' policies to protect students from outbursts of violence when differences of opinion were being expressed. All this had become indeed a sad reflection on the decline of free speech in what had been a proud free-thinking nation.

From the 1960s and on into the 80s, there was an increasing rate of economic decline. Textile mills had been closing at the rate of one per week between 1960 and 1970, to the extent that by 1980 the industry had all but disappeared. Heavy industry was also in decline with the result that the balance between those employed in manufacturing and those in services moved to an ever-increasing emphasis on services in the years ahead.

There were several factors which contributed to this decline. Failure to reinvest in the latest technologies and manufacturing techniques being one and compromise in quality to keep costs down to compete with completion in both the home and export markets certainly being another. The motor industry was the prime example. Also, however, from the 1960s, the trade unions began to 'flex their muscles', seeking better working conditions and wages, with some justification. This led to strike after strike which quickly began to undermine productive life in Britain. The miners were very much at the forefront, seeing their negotiating strength by being able to cut off the flow of coal, which was still the main source of energy for the nation. With coal prevented from restocking the power stations, the point was reached when the lights did really go out, it being necessary to restrict supply to industry to three days a week! Inflation peaked at 18% during this period. Britain became known as 'the Sick Man of Europe.' Things became so bad that the outlook led people with qualifications and ambition to leave the UK in droves for Canada, the USA as well as Australia and New Zealand. This became known as 'the Brain Drain.'

However, a new export industry was to burst onto the scene. Four boys from lower middle- and working-class backgrounds in Liverpool started producing pop music which was not only to become the rage in the UK, but in the USA and across the world. They were making a fortune, bringing in the dollars while proving that you could achieve that without having been to public school or university. To them, the class system was immaterial and so it became for others. The Beatles were exceptional musicians and entertainers and they made a very significant impact on society for the better for the future. While their most successful song released in 1965 was about unrequited love, had the lyric writer, Paul McCartney, been influenced consciously or subconsciously by the mood of the time? The song starts:

"Yesterday, all my troubles seemed so far away, now it looks as though they're here to stay, Oh I believe in yesterday." British pop music stormed the international market, think Rolling Stones, Elton John etc.

Meanwhile, Allotts' work on the Mexican power stations at Valle de México on the outskirts of Mexico City and at Salamanca, some one hundred miles to the north, went well being completed to time and budget. The dawn of the resurgence of Japanese heavy industry was becoming apparent.

38. Salamanca Power Station

105

At the outset of the projects, David with his K&D colleagues went to inspect the virgin site for the Salamanca plant. Standing in a remote field with just a very small substation to identify it was the correct site for the future power station, a car drew up; four small men got out. They looked Japanese.

"Are you consulting engineers for power station?"

"Yes."

"Ah so! We from Japanese company, Hitachi, we like to tender for turbine generators."

And they did; and won the contract with a very competitive price heavily subsidised by the Japanese government, which was helping exporters as the nation needed to build up its foreign currency reserves following defeat in the Second World War.

Allotts and K&D had opened a Mexico City liaison office in the Zona Rosa just off the Reforma Boulevard in the upmarket part of the city, walking distance from the Comisión Federal de Electricidad (CFE) offices. Bill Hoskinson, David's friend and to be James's godfather, was Allotts 'man in Mexico'.

Telephone communication between Mexico and the UK was very expensive; all transmission being by land and sub ocean cable. Satellite did not exist. The cheapest method was to have the message typed out in the office and take it to the Maria Isabel Intercontinental Hotel where the telephonist would prepare a punch tape of the message, which was fed into a machine that transmitted it quickly, keeping the cost to a minimum, as the message arrived in the Sale office as a telex. The fax machine had not been invented.

All Allotts' drawings and specifications were in Spanish, with a full-time translator employed in Sale office. David started to learn Spanish. He had not been good at languages at school, getting a zero mark in French dictation at O level! Nevertheless, he managed to achieve a level of fluency to offer to address the CFE in his Spanish at one of the progress meetings. By now, the Brits and

Mexicans were working very well together and he was encouraged to have a go. At the end of the session, the Mexicans said he had done well but in the future, they thought the meetings conducted in English would be the best idea! However, David could converse in Spanish with hotel and restaurant staff as well as taxi drivers. As they do, taxi drivers like a chat with their fares and in Mexico, the conversation would start:

"You Gringo (American)?"

"No, Ingles (English)." The reply from the taxi driver was certain to be:

"Ah! Manchester United, Bobby Charlton!"

39. David and Helga in Mexico

In 1968, Mr Ollier arranged for Helga to go with David to Mexico, which would be followed by a visit to Allott's office in Vancouver (Hansed Allott) where some of the design work for the Mexican power stations was being undertaken. They could then take a holiday visiting Helga's relatives in Kamloops, half way to the

Rockies.

They took the VC10 flight from Manchester to New York for an overnight stay there, just time to get a glimpse of the city. After visiting Mexico they travelled to Vancouver with a short stopover in San Francisco. With business done at Hansed Allotts, they took the train to Kamloops. There, Helga's aunt Betty Stockton lived with her son Rob, who had had a flying accident while serving in the Royal Canadian Air Force during the War and, to some extent, relied on his mother for support. Aunt Betty and Uncle Robert had staked out their land in 1923. Cousin Rob showed Helga and David around, including taking David fishing with some success.

Aunt Betty had two daughters, Nonie and Bet. Bet lived nearby with her husband, Roy, and three children. Roy was a doctor and the family lived well. David and Helga had a week experiencing the good life all Canadians took for granted. They had a weekend cabin on Nicola Lake, some forty miles from Kamloops, with a fishing boat and speedboat for water skiing. David and Helga determined they would create the same lifestyle in England. The only question was, how?

James was only two and spent the time his parents were away with his granny and granddad Postlethwaite who had retired to Springfield Farm, one of the houses on the Cross-family farms where Helga had lived in the early days of the War.

Helga had not been well before this trip, suffering from vertigo; it was brave of her to make the trip. However, it was hoped it would do her good. While she coped during the holiday, she was worse when she got back. It was so serious that David began to think she would not survive. However, after suffering for a year or two, she changed doctor and gave up the treatment she had been receiving, to soon recover. From then on, she enjoyed good health.

David's father and his new wife, Pat, had now settled down

in a cottage in the hills above Bolton. David and Helga wanted Pat to become a full part of James's family life. There were frequent visits to Granddad Compston and Auntie Pat, as she became known, for Sunday lunches. As grandparents do, James received special presents from them, delivered by Father Christmas, which included his favourite toy, a sit on three-wheel pedal tractor. Such was the respect in society for the secret of Father Christmas that even the BBC and other public entertainers never said anything that might compromise or spoil the belief children had in Father Christmas.

Judith, David's sister, married Graham Meare in 1967. Her father and Pat accepted the invitation to the wedding, also attended by her mother and her new husband, Ken Morley. He was a cold character and did not encourage visits by James. Consequently, James did not have the chance to bond with his Grandma Morley.

The World Cup was held in Mexico in 1970. England was the reigning world champion, coming to defend their title. They went first to acclimatise in Bogota in Colombia, being very high above sea level like Mexico City. Before leaving Bogota, their captain Bobby Moore was arrested, accused of trying to steal a bracelet from the jewellery shop in the hotel the team were staying in. He was retained in Bogota while the rest of the team moved on to Mexico City. By this time, Allotts' 'man in Mexico' was George Carpenter, who had become completely fluent in Spanish. He was mad keen on football and regularly was a guest of CFE in their box at the Azteca Stadium which was to be the main venue for the World Cup. He decided to see if he could be involved in helping the English squad while in Mexico and went to the British Embassy to offer his services. Clearly, football was not high on the agenda at the British Embassy. The World Cup was a matter for a very junior Third Secretary whose office was in the basement. George was directed there. Explaining he would be pleased to help if necessary while the English team were in Mexico, the Third Secretary replied in a very 'far back' snooty voice, "The World Cup football, I believe they play that with a round ball!" Not an encouraging start for George to become involved. However, the news that the British prime minister had been involved in pressing for Bobby Moore to be released to fly to Mexico for the competition, caused the British Embassy to take matters very seriously. Bobby Moore would fly into Mexico to be met by hordes of the world's press. The Embassy needed a man who was keen on football and spoke fluent Spanish to guide Moore through the airport full of pressmen and cameras and deliver him to the team hotel trying to avoid as much hassle as possible. The junior Third Secretary did not seem to be that man and such a job was beneath a senior diplomat, no doubt. After all, this was a 'working class' game! George got the call. If he was provided with an embassy car and driver, could he go to the airport to bring Bobby Moore to the team hotel? George was more than happy to oblige.

Off George set on the day Moore was due to land. The airport terminal building was small and did not have covered access to the aircraft, the aircraft standing on the tarmac apron with passengers descending steps from the aircraft and walking the short distance to the terminal building. George thought he somehow needed to get his embassy car to the bottom of those steps. He would have no problem recognising Bobby Moore, and the car flying the Union Jack with peak-capped chauffer would be what Moore might be expecting. George found the gate which opened onto the apron where the aircraft would come to a halt. There was a gateman at the gate. George set about 'chatting him up'. All Mexicans are mad about football, there was plenty to chat about. As the plane arrived, George explained he was from the British Embassy and had come to collect Bobby Moore, and if he could take the car up to the plane. The gateman asked to see his British Embassy identity card. George did not have one, but with a flash of quick thinking, he produced his blue RAC card which had a crown on it. The gateman not able to read English was impressed enough with the crown logo and let George and his car pass. Bobby Moore duly came straight down the steps from the aircraft into the car to be whisked away into Mexico City without the press even seeing him.

On the Saturday before the start of the World Cup competition, the England squad was invited to the Reforma Country Club on the outskirts of the city centre for a relaxing day. The other England squad in Mexico was also invited, being the Allott K&D power station men. In the afternoon, the England football team played the Reforma Club at cricket. The footballers proved to be good at cricket and won by mid-afternoon. George Carpenter, by now well known to the England squad, challenged them to a game of football and they accepted, no doubt expecting to win! And they did. David was in goal and reported the ball seemed to go straight through him when they shot on target!

In the evening, there were two mixed teams that played a darts match. David was in Alf Ramsey, the England manager's team. This was followed by a good English dinner with food brought in from England.

At the end of the 1960s, Uncle Sandy sold the Scafell Hotel and his other property in Rosthwaite. After a year or so, he moved to Auchencairn on the Solway Coast in Dumfries, Scotland. Now, David and Helga no longer had a 'bolt-hole' to go to in the Lake District. So, they bought a twenty-foot cabin cruiser to be moored on Ullswater, named *Lindy*. David also shared a clinker-built rowing boat used for fishing kept at the Lyths Tower boathouse near Aira

Force also on Ullswater. All they needed now to match the Canadian good life was a holiday home near the lake. However, they certainly did not have the money to buy one. So, *MV Lindy* became their holiday home for the next three years.

On top of all Helga's other duties, she was appointed executor for her two Stockton aunts, Emily and Doris, who had been committed to hospital suffering from a form of dementia. The younger aunt, Doris, lived in the hospital for seventeen years. During this period, Helga managed her aunts' finances, increasing the value from £4,500 to £48,000. A professional fund manager would have been proud of that!

On Doris's death without a will, Helga and the family solicitors arranged for this money to be distributed to the correct members of the family in the UK and Canada, she herself not being in line to receive any. She undertook this task refusing any expenses or fee for her services, as she did for many other tasks on behalf of the older members of the family in the years ahead. She saw such action as a duty and pleasure.

Thus, with Helga's unstinting efforts to maintain a routine of life based in Stonegate Cottage and being organised for the family to go away at weekends and for holidays in the Lake District and North Yorkshire, a balancing act had been established for international business life to sit comfortably with a full family life in the UK.

Allotts carried out a number of additional commissions for the CFE in Mexico while the two power stations were under construction. However, when CFE decided to add a further extension at Valle de Mexico, Bechtel, the huge American engineering company which had been the engineers for Phase 1, were determined to beat K&D/Allotts for this next extension. They offered to do all the design in Mexico, an offer the UK team could not match. So, the work in Mexico for Allotts came to an end.

David was promoted to associate (senior manager just below partner) in 1971, becoming responsible for one of the company's design and planning offices in Sale. Within a year, there was to be an upheaval in the Allott story.

CHAPTER TEN
A Step up on the Allott Ladder – Then Merger

In 1972, there was a significant upheaval in the Allott story. It was announced that the company was to merge with C. J. Lomax & Son, another Manchester- based long- established consulting engineers. They specialised in public health engineering, drainage and sewage treatment, with most of their work being in north-west England. The merged company became Allott & Lomax, with two of the Lomax partners, Jack Hill and Rodney Foster, joining the Allott partners to head up the new firm. David retained his position of associate in the new practice. Roger Hyde was now a partner. Allott & Lomax was shortly to become a limited liability company with shareholding directors instead of partners.

There was some element of imbalance in the business between the two companies which had merged. One now an international business dealing in complex major projects, i.e. fossil fuelled and nuclear power stations, the other with a north of England workload on rather smaller projects.

Nevertheless, for David and his Allott colleagues, the future would be Allott & Lomax.

The focus of David's work now moved away from power stations; this work now came under Roger Hyde. The company needed to diversify further. The massive programme in building new power stations in the UK was coming to an end. One such project remained, being Kilroot in Northern Ireland, which was ready to go ahead with K&D and Allotts appointed the consultants and for which Roger would take charge of the Allott work.

David's office became involved in industrial projects, with clients including Reckitt & Colman, Watney Mann and Courtaulds.

Courtaulds, at the time, were the leading British textile company and had plans for a significant investment in new manufacturing plant in Ireland. This would involve a man-made fibre process plant in Letterkenny in the Irish Republic, which would supply the new Courtauld textile mill just over the border near Londonderry, locally known as Derry. The mill was planned to cover all the processes from spinning yarn to final products of bedding linen. David spotted a report on the proposed project in *THE WALL STREET JOURNAL* and Allotts were appointed architects and engineers for the mill buildings. Although the mill was completed, even with the most up to date production facilities, Courtaulds could not compete with Asian imports and the factory never came into full production.

With Kilroot Power Station in Protestant territory and the Londonderry (Derry) mill in Catholic territory, Allotts were operating on both sides of the political divide.

The IRA campaign of terrorism was at its most active throughout this period. Fortunately, the impact on Allotts work was very limited.

Nevertheless, the Londonderry project experienced two incidents. Those attending the progress meeting one Christmas, on returning to site after lunch were greeted by a rather alarmed site general foreman. He reported that during the lunch break there had been an IRA armed robbery of the wages to be paid to the men at the end of the day. The men were all from the Bogside in Derry. Apparently on returning home in the evening, the IRA would pay them half of their wages, a nice Christmas bonus! Also, it was good PR for the IRA! The other half would go to IRA funds. Of course, the next day, the men would receive their full wages from their employer.

David was very concerned that large sums of cash were on site each pay day and instructed that wages must be paid by cheques in future. The following year on the December wages day, the IRA raided the little local bank near the site, as they knew it would be well stocked with cash to pay out the men from the site coming with their wages cheques.

A few months later, the restaurant used for lunches on progress meeting days was blown up by the IRA; happily, it was not a progress meeting day!

Allotts were involved in preparing proposals for a new university at Kebangsaan near Kuala Lumpur, Malaya. George Carpenter was the Allott man working with the planners' team in Kuala Lumpur. The project would require the support of the prime minister, a keen golfer, if it was to go ahead. It was decided that a golf course must be included on the university campus. As the work was nearing completion, the golf course designer had not arrived. George was the only golfer in the planning team and was put to work designing the golf course. He used a Hawkstone Park GC scorecard he had with him as a template. The scheme met the prime minister's approval with the university being built, including George's golf course. George went on to design other golf courses including one in Spain.

David's staff worked in open-plan offices, each person having a large desk on which full-sized engineering drawings could be laid out, with a drawing board alongside. The electronic handheld calculator had been launched in 1960 and by the mid 1970s the pocket-sized versions were available. The days when engineers used the slide rule for their calculations had come to an end. Allotts invested in a computer for complicated engineering calculations as well as a management tool. It was quite large and located in an air-conditioned room with a small specialised staff to operate it. Personal computers, laptops, never mind tablets, were years into the future. In the main, all drawings were done by hand.

Meanwhile, in family life, James was now attending the very small Arley village school. There were two teachers for the pupils with ages from five to eleven. The school had a good academic record. It was in a beautiful black and white timbered building within the private area of the Arley Estate.

With the Scafell Hotel no longer in the family, time in the Lake District was limited to weekends and holidays on *MV Lindy*. Then in 1973, opportunity for having a holiday home there arose. While there had been dreams of having a holiday home to go with the boats on Ullswater, matching the Canadian lifestyle of Bet and Roy, David and Helga certainly had no money to buy one. It was David's mother, who also loved the Lake District, where she had been brought up at the Scafell Hotel, who had seen an advertisement in *THE DAILY TELEGRAPH* for a cottage to rent on Lord Lonsdale's Lowther Estate near Penrith. The cottage would need to be renovated by the leaser. She brought this to David and Helga's attention.

Lord Lonsdale's agent was Derrick Pattinson, a friend of Uncle Sandy. Through this friendship, David had got to know Derrick and they would go fishing together on Derrick's boat on Ullswater.

With no intention of renting the cottage, but feeling they should show some reaction to David's mother's interest, they thought it would make a good day out if they went to see the cottage. Accordingly, they rang Derrick to ask if they could see the cottage. He invited them to his office on the Lowther Estate.

40. Whale Moore Bothy

They called to collect the key. "Oh, there is no key, the place is not habitable, just go in. It is used as a shelter by the shepherds."

Using David's building knowledge, David and Helga went to have a look over the place and returned to thank Derrick for letting them have a look.

"What do you think?" asked Derrick.

"Well, I think the roof line is good and the building seems weather tight, so it should make a nice little home," David replied.

"Good, that settles it," said Derrick. "Lord Lonsdale will be very pleased we have found a tenant whom we know from all the two hundred and fifty responses we have had from the advertisement in The *TELEGRAPH*."

"You mean us?" David and Helga asked. But how could they possibly afford it, they thought.

"What would be the upfront key money and how much would the rent be?"

"There is no key so there is no key money to pay. How about a rent of £2 per week plus tuppence for the outside earth closet?"

This was too good a chance to miss and they accepted there and then. There would be a rent review every seven years. However, there never was for all the time they had the cottage until they gave up the lease eleven and a half years later.

David and Helga managed to obtain a local authority grant to install a water supply, bathroom and WC together with a septic tank, and with a bit more borrowing, set about the

41. MV Lindy on Ullswater

renovation. Whale Moor Bothy, as it was to be called, became a three-bedroomed house with kitchen, dining room, sitting room and bathroom with WC. There was a small garden at the front, just big enough to keep the bull from the front door. It became for the Compstons and their friends, especially the Kents, a holiday base for the next eleven years.

However, the renovations had to be completed in the first year of the lease if the local authority grant was to be paid.

Accordingly, with only the internal doors to paint, the rest of the work being completed, the building inspector was asked to inspect the work so the grant could be approved by the deadline of

42. James' Fireball on Ullswater

the end of the local authority financial year on 5th April. He announced he could not give his approval until the doors were painted. There was just a week to the deadline.

MV Lindy was launched at the earliest date covered by the insurance, 1st April. This was

119

to be Helga's base from which she would go and paint the doors, while David was blissfully going to the office in Sale each day from the comfort of Stonegate Cottage! The work was completed in time and the only criticism Helga received for her work was from one of the shepherds, "You are putting the paint on upside down!"

James started prep boarding school at St Hugh's in Woodhall Spa in Lincolnshire in 1973. It had been chosen because David had gone there. A school in Cheshire would have been a more sensible plan. Being so far away certainly deprived Helga of a day to day relationship with her only child, he being so far away in term times. Nevertheless, James did well at St Hugh's. School fees were now a significant part of the budget, and David felt the need to explore the possibility of a good increase in his income. Positions with both W. S. Atkins and Montreal Engineering in Canada were potentially on offer, enough to drop a hint to Allotts. Sometimes a little subtle pressure by simply asking for a reference is enough to tactfully make a point. The point David was making was that he now wanted a promotion. Promotion meant becoming a director and that meant providing some capital if he were invited to join the Board.

The response was very positive from the chairman, Mr Ollier. There was some negotiation as to the value of the shares on offer to David. However, as it happened, the business was passing through a difficult period at that time. Advised by his old school friend, Graham Elliott, who by now had his own accountancy practice in Manchester, a good deal was struck and David obtained a loan from his bank to buy the shares. So, in 1975, he became a director of Allott & Lomax. He knew the former C. S. Allott & Son partners welcomed him joining them on the Board. Rodney Foster told him, "It was a bit early"!

"All work and no play makes Jack a dull boy," as the saying

goes. There is no doubt that there was to be no shortage of pressure at work for David. However, with Helga's efforts during the weekdays running the Stonegate Cottage home base including keeping the garden immaculate, and her forward catering planning, on most Friday nights, they set off for Whale Moor Bothy to relax in Cumbria, often spending time on *MV Lindy* on Ullswater as well as fell walking. David had access to fishing on the River Lowther in the valley down from Whale Moor.

They bought Stonegate Cottage from Lord and Lady Ashbrook at the end of a major foot and mouth outbreak in the farm animals in Shropshire, North Wales and Cheshire in 1976. Uncle Sandy loaned them the deposit on fair terms to both parties with defined interest and an agreed term over which the loan would be paid off. Getting a mortgage had proved to be another thing!

Most mortgages were provided by building societies as far as David and Helga could see. However, building societies only had very limited cash resources and there were severe limitations on what they had available to lend. David and Helga were not 'worldly wise' when it came to raising finance. They decided they would ask the Abbey National Building Society for the mortgage they needed. When the lady manager in the Sale branch was told it was for an old cottage which had just been renovated, she was far from impressed; they did not lend on old properties.

Helga said she thought this unreasonable, particularly as she was the executor of her aunt's estate and had invested some of those funds in the Abbey National and was therefore, to all intents and purposes, an existing customer. Indeed, it was for this reason they had chosen to approach the Abbey National for the mortgage. In these circumstances, Helga said she would withdraw the investment she controlled. The manager asked for the details of the account Helga controlled and then went into the back office. The manager reappeared with a smile on her face, no doubt having established Helga had invested for her aunt more than the mortgage being asked for. The Abbey National would be only too pleased to provide the mortgage.

Helga's Canadian cousin, Bet, with husband Roy came to stay. She brought with her a scrap of notebook paper on which was typed, "HISTORY OF STOCKTONS." This had been sent to Bet's sister Nonie by a friend Nonie had met at a Canadian air force get-together. Nonie and her friend, Barbara, discovered they were related.

There were all sorts of references to Stocktons who had ranked as 'the great and good' of their times, crusaders, knights and a Lord Mayor of London. However, the most documented and plausible was the reference to a John Stockton from Cheshire who emigrated to America in 1660 and whose grandson, Richard, signed the Declaration of Independence.

Could it be that Helga, whose mother was a Stockton, was of the same family line as a signer of the Declaration of Independence?

HISTORY OF STOCKTON'S

- 700 years history
- Crusaders, knights and Lord Mayor of London 1470-1 ranking in those days next to the king.
- Richard Stockton signed the declaration of Independence in the U.S.A.
- Rt. Hon. John Stockton, Lord Mayor of London - a son of Richard Stockton who was knighted on the field by King Edward IV.
- Sir Edward Stockton, vicar of Cookham in Berkshire was leader of one of the early expeditions to the Holy Land.
- In the 12th century Stocktons were Lords of the Manor of Stockton which they held under the barony of Malpas. Stockton Manor is in the county of Cheshire.
- David Stockton inherited the Manor of Stockton from his father in 1250.
- The beginning of the American Stockton's was with Richard, the son of John Stockton of the parish of Malpas. He settled in Flushing in 1660
- Richard his son, located at Princeton University and the town proper.
- Richard the Signer was his son.
- Richard the Duke, a son of Richard the Signer.
- Fighting Bob - a son of Richard the Duke is known to history as Commodore Robert Field Stockton. He was a student at Princeton when only 13 years of age. A few years later he left to enter the navy. After 10 years in foreign countries he became interested in the American Colonization Scheme and he established a colony on the west coast of Africa which subsequently became the Republic of Liberia.
- In 1842 he constructed a steamship of war armed with 12 - 42 pounders and 2 guns, 10 tons each which were called the "Peacemaker" and the "Oregon". Commodore Stockton was the means of establishing a civil government over California before the Mexican War closed.
- He resigned his command in 1849, in 1851 he was elected to the Senate in New Jersey. To him is due the construction of the Delaware and Raritan Canal and of the Camden and Amboy Railroad.
- Philip Augustus Stockton was also a naval hero. He served on the old "Constitution" when it was the flagship of Commodore Read. He resigned with the rank of lieutenant and was Consul General of Saxony for 6 years.
- Commodore Stockton had 3 sons - Richard, John Potter and General Robert Field Stockton.
- Morven - is the old Stockton residence. It was one of the celebrated houses of America. It has been the home of the Stocktons for over 200 years and stands today in the most picturesque part of Princeton. General Washington stayed there.
- Name was written "De Stockton" in Primitive days and in later times Stockton: the only change the name has undergone during a period of at least 800 years.

43. History of the Stocktons

CHAPTER ELEVEN
David and Helga: "Who do you think you are?"

David and Helga had lived far apart until they met in their early twenties at the sports clubs in Sale. The longer they knew each other, they found their backgrounds had more and more in common. Their wedding guests had included Helga's godmother, Hilda Brighouse, and David's granny, Clara Badrock. Although they had not seen each other for many years, they had known each other very well in the 1930s when Hilda was a regular guest at the Badrock's Scafell Hotel in the Lake District.

Having been born in the Lake District, David was proud of being a Cumbrian. Helga's father was born in Carlisle, his family, the Postlethwaites, had deep roots in Cumbria. Helga had three Postlethwaite aunts who had lived in Keswick and who knew David's Uncle Sandy. The Postlethwaites had left a mark in Cumberland. Helga's grandfather, John James Postlethwaite, played bowls in Carlisle and was the all-England lawn bowls singles champion in 1911. Her great-uncle, John Postlethwaite, was born in 1840. Although he was a railwayman by profession, being a chartered mechanical engineer and a manager on the Penrith to Cockermouth railway, he became a distinguished amateur geologist being the author of *POSTLETHWAITE'S MINES AND MINING IN THE ENGLISH LAKE DISTRICT*. First published in 1877, there was a second enlarged edition in 1889, a third edition in 1913, then again in 1975, this last being a 'best-seller'. As a mark of the respect he

Helga and David became members of the Stockton Society in 1999. There could not have been a better time to join. After attending the 1999 annual meeting, as always, held in Bunbury, in the following year, being the Millennium, members came to the annual meeting from the USA, Canada and Australia to meet up with the UK members. Direct descendants of 'the Signer', Richard Stockton, were present. Within the next year, Helga's family line was traced back to Thomas Stockton born in about 1552 and buried in Malpas near Bunbury in Cheshire in 1606.

45. Robert Stockton
'The Art Dealer'

The Americans had the history of 'the Signer's' line. It was 'the Signer's' great-grandfather, Richard Stockton, who had emigrated to America from Cheshire in about 1658, settling in Flushing, now part of the New York conurbation. He became known in family circles as 'The Emigrant'. His son, who had been born in Malpas, Cheshire, moved to Princeton and became known as 'The Princeton Settler'. The Stocktons went on to establish a prosperous living from the land round Princeton, with 'The Princeton Settler's' son, John, giving land for the establishment of Princeton College which was to become Princeton University. The family originally built a stone Cheshire-style cottage, The Barracks, still there as a private house less than a mile from the University. John's son was Richard

'The Signer'. The family had built a splendid plantation style residence, Morven, just 'a stone's throw' from The Barracks. It was to become a museum of the Stocktons' role in the development of Princeton and the family's part in American history.

46. "The Baracks
Princeton, NJ

47. "Morven"
Princeton, NJ

Sadly the personal and business papers of 'The Signer' were stolen or destroyed by the British during the Revolutionary War occupation of Princeton.

Richard Stockton 'The Emigrant' made a dramatic impact on the family history by moving from Cheshire to America thus founding a family dynasty there which was to include Stocktons who have contributed to the development of the United States and taken their places in its history, well documented in the book published in 2004, *MORVEN – MEMORY, MYTH AND REALITY* by Constance M Greiff and Wanda S Gunning, nevertheless, stating "The English origins of the (Stockton) family have never been established precisely."

Richard 'The Signer' had a son Richard, known as 'The Duke'. He was a lawyer and served in the United States Congress. However, it was his son, Robert Field Stockton, who played a role in the history of the USA to compliment that of his grandfather 'The Signer'. Robert Field Stockton became a commodore in the US Navy. He saw action in the war of 1812, being promoted to lieutenant for his part in the defence of Baltimore. His bravery and zest for battle earned him the nick-name 'Fighting Bob.' Later, sailing to Africa in command of the *USN ALLIGATOR*, he discovered a desirable piece of land on a cape 600 miles from the British colony of Sierra Leone. In negations with the local ruler, he obtained the land that has become Liberia.

On his father's death in 1828, 'Fighting Bob' became involved in a project which had long been an interest to his father, the proposal to construct a canal linking the Delaware and Raritan rivers. 'Fighting Bob' and his father-in-law provided at least half of the capital to build the canal, which was to prove a financial success.

48. The Declaration of Independence by John Trumbull
(Robert Stockton seated at far back to the right of the five standing)

In 1845 war with Mexico imminent. Posted first to Texas and then being appointed commodore of the US Navy Pacific Fleet, 'Fighting Bob' arrived in Monterey to meet up with Captain John Charles Fremont. Together, they planned the conquest of California resulting in the surrender of the Mexican Californians in January 1847. The city of Stockton in California is named after the family.

Some years earlier in 1838 in England another Stockton, Robert, 'Robert the Walker', at the age of seventeen walked away from his native village of Bunbury the thirty-five miles to find a more challenging life in 'Cottonopolis' (Manchester). Likewise, he pioneered the change in the fortunes of the English Stockton branch.

Robert 'The Walker' was born in May 1821, being one of the younger sons, Joseph Stockton of Bunbury. He had six brothers and five sisters. Although living in a beautiful part of Cheshire, there was limited opportunity for good employment in the village which had very limited resources at a time of great industrial development in the towns and cities. He had worked since the age of ten or eleven in service at Spurston Hall, a mile from Bunbury. It was in Dick Whittington fashion that he set off on his walk to Cottonopolis. While he was leaving his family and roots behind, he did have an older sister, Martha, who by now lived at Irlam O' Th' Heights near Manchester. Passing initially through woods and forest, he came to parkland on Lord Egerton's estate of Tatton, when thereafter the road into Manchester improved. On the way through Sale, he found employment before going on to find his sister. There, he found temporary employment with Sir Elkanah Armitage who introduced him to Sir Robert Peel, famous for creating the first police force, "the Peelers."

Now moving in the right circles, Robert obtained a position in the engineers' department of the Lancashire & Yorkshire Railway

Company, where he worked for many years.

Robert 'The Walker' had made the transmission from 'country lad' to a 'city worker' involved in the great Industrial Revolution of the Victorian Era. He was the father of thirteen children, the oldest boy Edwin the father of Sir Edwin Stockton, the industrialist, Robert Stockton, the art dealer, and Helga's grandfather, James Arthur Stockton. Robert 'The Walker' died at the age of sixty-seven in March 1889.

Sir Edwin Stockton, Helga's great-uncle, was a successful industrialist, who lived in Sale in Priory Park and later moved to Jodrell Hall, where part of his estate was to become the site for the Jodrell Bank radio telescope. Amongst his directorships, he was on the board of directors of the Manchester Ship Canal Company, reflecting an involvement in inland waterways as had his distant cousin, 'Fighting Bob', in America. Helga's Great-Uncle Robert gave "Fifty Years of Friendship and Devoted Service" to Thomas Agnew & Sons, the famous London art dealers, being presented a gold watch in memory of this in 1929.

Putting together the American and the English lines of the Stocktons, both with a focal point on Bunbury/Malpas area of Cheshire, there was now compelling evidence that they were of a common family line. However, there were two uncertain links. Was Richard Stockton baptised in 1675 in the parish of Bunbury the son of Thomas Stockton of Malpas baptised in 1636? It seemed most likely but no records had been found to prove it. 'The Emigrant's' father, John, was baptised in Malpas in 1609. Thomas of Malpas was baptised in Malpas in 1606. Could he and John be cousins or even brothers? It seems quite probable they were one or the other. If so, their father or grandfather would represent the earliest common ancestor between the American branch and the English branch of the family. Likewise, there was just the possibility Richard 'the Emigrant's' father might not be the John from Malpas. However, since his son 'the Princeton Settler' was recorded as born in Malpas, it seemed practically certain 'the Emigrant' was from the same line as Thomas Stockton of Malpas. Likewise, the records for absolute proof had not been found. The question remained, could it be proved without doubt that Helga was from the same family line as 'the Signer'?

The Americans were just as interested in finding out with which UK Stocktons they shared a common ancestor. The only way to be certain of this became possible with the development of DNA science. However, this required an unbroken male line from the late 1500s to living males in America and the UK now in 2008. If Helga's cousin, Ken Stockton, the treasurer of The Stockton Family Society, had DNA that matched the American direct descendants of 'the Signer', then he and Helga were of the same family line as 'the Signer.' Many Stocktons on both sides of the Atlantic agreed to DNA testing.

In 2006, Helga and David visited Princeton to go to the Stockton museum in Morven. By now, they were confident that the compelling evidence showed Helga had a common ancestor with 'the Signer.' They had explained to the curator before the visit the family link and therefore the special reason for their visit. They had booked to have afternoon tea at Morven during their planned visit. On arrival, Helga was greeted as a long-lost member of the family and quickly ushered to join a tour of the museum which had just started. "Ladies and gentlemen," the curator started, interrupting the tour guide. "We have a very special visitor today. May I introduce Helga of the Stockton family in Cheshire England." The response was wide mouthed Americans, "Gee! You are one of the English Stocktons are you!" Helga had never felt like royalty before or since, but she did for a moment or two then. She must have made that tour group's day!

When the DNA results became known, they showed that Helga's cousin Ken had a close match to the American descendants of 'the Signer.' The direct family link between Helga and 'the Signer' had been established.

Later, in 2017, more extensive testing of Helga's relation William Edwin 'Bill' Stockton's DNA showed the probable common ancestor in the range of twelve generations. *See image of family tree opposite.*

It had been intriguing and fun research. And again, David and Helga had found another common link in their backgrounds though the Badrock and Stockton families both going back to origins in Bunbury/Malpas.

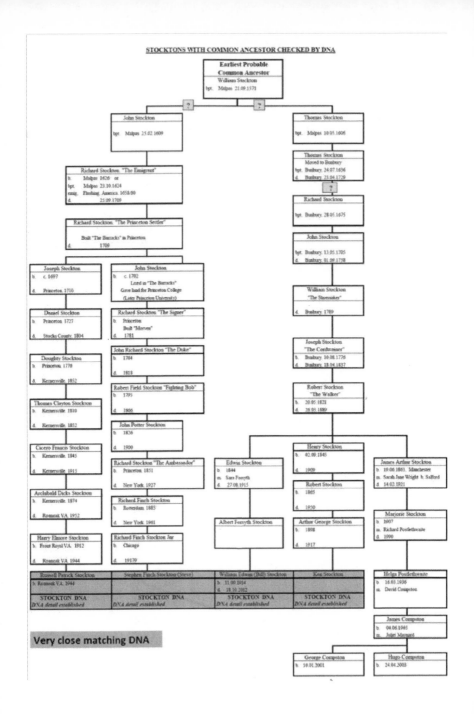

STOCKTONS WITH COMMON ANCESTOR CHECKED BY DNA

Very close matching DNA

50. Robert Stockton 'The Signer'

51. The Declaration of Independence

CHAPTER TWELVE
Exporting Matters, so does "Keeping the Home Fires Burning"

When David became a director of Allott & Lomax in 1975, the challenges facing the company were quite severe. The end of the CEGB's programme for the construction of very large fossil-fuelled power stations was in sight. Allotts had had a continuous workload, involving the greater part of their staff, on this programme since 1961.

The UK economy was in serious decline. The Labour government had become hostage to the trade unions, which called strike after strike which were achieving nothing short of driving the country to ruin. The miners were in the forefront leading this chaos. This resulted in power stations being deprived of coal to the point that in January to March 1974, there was such a shortage of available electricity generating capacity that industry was reduced to a three-day working week. Britain had become known as "the Sick Man of Europe."

The UK was desperate for a powerful leader to take a grip of the disruption being caused by the trade unions while engendering a new mood of a strong work ethic within the population. Such leadership was not going to be found in the Labour Party, the government of the day.

Beyond the shores of Great Britain, the world was changing fast. In 1973, the UK joined the European Common Market (EEC). Helga expressed the view that, "it will never work." In 2015, the Greek economic crisis followed by chaos caused by the ease of movement of refugees throughout mainland Europe were proving her right, a view shared by the UK population in 2016 who voted 'Brexit' to leave the EU.

Chinese economic reform started in 1978, heralding the beginning of the dramatic rebalancing of the world economies during the rest of David's and Helga's lives.

The UK suffered 'the Winter of Discontent' in 1978 when the public-sector workers' strike stopped rubbish collections with garbage piled up in town and city streets, even gravediggers were on strike.

52. The Winter of Discontent

For Allotts, this meant that finding business largely based on work in the UK was not a good option. Lin Ollier, as chairman of the company, grasped the challenge and turned attention to expanding into overseas markets. The leading London-based consulting engineers had always been active overseas going back to the time of building the infrastructure for the British Empire. Allotts up to this time had relied on the home market for most of its business. The strategy now was to penetrate the markets in the world where there was oil and money. This meant the Middle East and Nigeria.

In addition to his responsibilities for managing a planning and design department in head office, David and co-director Mike Sargent were given the task of breaking into these markets.

In 1975, practically half of the firm's business was still involved in the planning and design for power stations with similar work for the industrial sector representing another 17.5% of work. That is to say, two thirds of the work was coming from only two sectors in the UK economy, both of which were in decline.

While David was regularly travelling to Mexico on business in the late 60s and early 70s, he tried to obtain work from Standard Oil of California. The company was planning to build a large refinery on the Firth of Clyde. David had established a good relationship with Standard Oil's project team based in San Francisco, when unfortunately, Standard Oil decided to pull out of the project with the prospect of a long drawn-out public enquiry looming.

It was on David's first visit to San Francisco on the Sunday before his first meeting with Standard Oil that he went down to Fisherman's Wharf. It was still a working fishing port with many trawlers and other fishing craft as well as a wharf side fish market, much like Whitby in England. However, there was a salmon fishing boat trip advertised. Fishing poles (rods) could be hired for the trip and live anchovy hooked through their heads would be provided as bait. Although dressed in his business suit, David decided to take the fishing trip. Sue and Paul Consolo were also on board with packed lunches. They chatted to David and realised he had gone on the spur of the moment completely unprepared to go to sea fishing. They kindly shared their packed lunch with him. Sue, who married twice after, became a lifelong friend to David and Helga, over the years they visited each other's homes and took many holidays together in the UK, Europe and America. By the way, no salmon was caught on that trip!

The experience of marketing Allotts to a major American corporation proved invaluable to David for the future. While trying to obtain the work from Standard Oil, David had bought a book on sale in America. *MARKETING ARCHITECTURAL AND ENGINEERING SERVICES.* At this time, the rules of the governing bodies of professional practices in the UK banned the soliciting of new business, that is to say, marketing and sales approaches to possible new clients, including taking part in competitive tendering. Clients were expected to come and ask for the services they required, choosing those they approached based on the reputation of the firm. In America, there were certainly no such hang-ups, whether it was about selling Mars Bars or getting a contract on a refinery project.

Nevertheless, despite the restrictive code of conduct relating to securing business as a professional engineering practice, it was clear to Lin Ollier, David and Mike Sargent that such restrictions would have to be ignored if Allotts were to penetrate new markets in the Middle East and Nigeria.

It was on the 19th January 1975 that Lin Ollier and David had set off for Lagos in Nigeria. Although Lin had served as an officer in the West African Frontier Force in the Far East in World War Two, neither he nor David had any real knowledge of Nigeria. However, they were to meet up in Lagos with Ayo Akideinde, a former member of Allotts staff in England and Professor Royston Jones from Nairobi, a friend of Lin's.

Lin and David established a company with Ayo Akideinde, to be known as Akideinde Allott & Lomax (Nigeria) Ltd. The company made a good start with contact being made with Colonel Murtala Mohammed, commanding officer of the Nigerian Army Signals Regiment. Nigeria was under military rule. Oil revenues had resulted in a boom of local wealth with Nigerians spending a large slice of the revenue on cars, and, by the way, on champagne! Since the telephone system was completely unreliable, people used their cars when they needed to contact one another, either on business or private matters. Consequently, the road system in Lagos was gridlocked.

The military government decided a priority was to repair the telephone cable network, a task to be undertaken by the Signals Regiment, an organisation that had very limited knowledge or skill for such a massive job. Allotts were asked if they might help. Fortunately, Allotts' personnel director was Colonel Bishop, a former commanding officer of the Royal Engineers, in which Col Mohammed had spent time during his training. Dick Bishop was dispatched with all speed to Lagos to meet Colonel Mohammad.

The two colonels got on like a house on fire and Allotts were appointed to help the Nigerian Signals Regiment rebuild the telephone network. Allotts had never done such a job before, however, Colonel Bishop with true military wartime emergency planning and management soon had a team trained and in Nigeria to get the job done. And it was!

From this start the business expanded, with Ted Bielinski as general manager, going on to undertake the planning and design of new trunk roads, industrial plants and structural engineering. Ted had worked for Allotts for many years. His family had been refugees from Poland during World War Two finishing up in East Africa, Ted then being old enough to help the family make a living. He was therefore 'an African Hand'. An office was opened on the Lagos Waterfront with several regional offices. One of the most prestigious projects undertaken by the Lagos office staff was the structural design for the then tallest building in West Africa, the Chellerams Building on the Marina Waterfront in Lagos.

The company has prospered to the time of writing in 2015, changing hands but still in business now known as Allott (Nigeria) Ltd.

David also now had the opportunity to secure work in Kuwait. The World Bank had recommended Allotts to the National Industries Company of Kuwait which had been entrusted by the Emir with the task of establishing a new industrial sector based on exploiting local recourses to help to diversify the economy which was practically entirely based on oil exporting and refining.

Allotts were successful in being appointed as consulting engineers for a new large lime-making and sand lime brick plant. Dieter Deffner, a consulting engineer from Germany, was already appointed as the process engineering consultant. Allotts secured other work from the National Industries Company (NIC) during the next few years.

53. With Kuwaiti clients

Peter Hardy worked closely with David as the project manager on the work in Kuwait, acting with David in a double act in negotiations leading to new contracts. Peter played 'the hard man' with David joining in the negotiations to close the deals by providing the discount that the chairman of NIC was looking for.

The art was to finish up by not giving away the entire discount which had been allowed for in the original tender price! Similar projects to those in Kuwait, followed working with Dieter Deffner in Jordan and Nepal.

The relationship between Dieter and David led to Allotts having offices in Germany. Inkoplan was established being each half owned by Allotts and Heitkamp, a large family owned German construction group.

Dieter became the manager with the head office in Essen and several years later joined the board of directors of Allott & Lomax (Holdings) Ltd.

With David now turning his attention increasingly to export business, the Compstons, David, Helga and James, were to find themselves each following rather different life experiences for many years ahead.

However, they were bonded together by Helga with a home lifestyle based on Stonegate Cottage in Cheshire and with their Lake District 'bolt-hole' at Whale Moor Bothy.

James had started boarding school at St Hugh's in Woodhall Spa in Lincolnshire a year and a half before David became a director of Allott & Lomax. Once David became a director, he spent much of his time travelling abroad on short business trips, in total, spending up to half of the nights in a year

54. Stonegate Cottage with James aged 2

away from home. It fell to Helga to take James to and from school at the beginning and end of terms and for exiats, one each term.

This involved a drive of one hundred and twenty-five miles each way from Cheshire to Woodhall Spa in Lincolnshire. On reflection, it was perhaps not sensible to have sent James so far away from home to school at seven and a half.

Helga was certainly very upset when she first left him there, as indeed, as was to be expected, was James. However, he soon settled down and fitted in, enjoying life at St Hugh's. He did well academically and easily passed his 'common entrance' exams for Mill Hill School in north-west London in 1978.

It was while James was at St Hugh's that Helga began to play a corporate entertainment role in support of Allott & Lomax. Initially, this involved looking after the wife of a client from Nigeria when she visited England to see her children at boarding schools. As a non-driver, Helga would take her to the schools. Helga also started to act as a hostess at dinner functions in London attended by clients as guests of the firm.

At the end of James's time at St Hugh's, the family had a trip to Nigeria to experience life as expats for a few weeks. This was followed by a holiday in Kenya.

Nigeria really opened James's eyes to the gulf in living standards between the UK and the developing Third World.

55. Living the expat life

Arriving in Nairobi, the family had some misgivings. The head of state, Jomo Kenyatta, had just died. He had been an excellent leader of the country since independence, now would there be immediate unrest?

However, all was peaceful on arrival at the airport with a stark contrast to Nigeria evident at once with the red carpets to the kerbside taxi ranks and the spotless streets on the way to the beautifully maintained and excellently run old colonial-style Norfolk Hotel. The time in Kenya was well spent, including a safari visit to Tree Tops and a game park outing with a private hire car and driver.

56. James ready for Mill Hill School

Starting at Mill Hill in the autumn term, James found himself one of only a very few who had already been to boarding school, quickly settling in and showing the others what the form was.

Helga's guiding hand was there to watch James's school progress throughout the rest of his school years. He did well at O level. He was good at English and languages. However, he chose a science base of subjects for A level. The outcome was disappointing. His mother acted, arranging for James to attend private tuition with some A level results being achieved. Nevertheless, James certainly must have learnt the science he was taught at Mill Hill, which was not reflected in his exam results there, as his successful career in the oil, power and resources sectors must have been founded on his science based learning at school. His London school background was perhaps more important in the context of the social environment of which he became part, making him completely at ease with the business environment in London from where he later established his international career.

After a brief time in his own business after leaving school, James joined the staff of Allott & Lomax, working in the archives. He went on to becoming a chartered member of the Institute of Marketing, working in the sales and marketing department of the company.

While James was at Mill Hill School, Helga's parents had moved to North Yorkshire at Springfield Farm, rented from the Cross family with whom Helga had spent her very early childhood during World War Two. So, during the years of driving from Cheshire to Woodhall Spa and then to Mill Hill in North London, Helga regularly visited her parents. The old farmhouse needed a going over, particularly decorating, Helga doing much of this for them.

Helga had a good friend who lived on the outskirts of Leeds, another calling place on her travels. Consequently, she became a good navigator. She had always been a good driver.

Family life in these circumstances can only survive if there is a person to 'keep the home fires burning.' Helga was that person; she looked after the garden at Stonegate, ran the domestic economics, paying the bills, while planning ahead so that weekend breaks and holidays could be taken at Whale Moor Bothy as often as possible.

In 1979, the change needed in the direction of UK politics came about with the election resulting in Margaret Thatcher becoming prime minister. The country was down and practically out. Thatcher set about encouraging business with a significant emphasis on exporting. Those travelling abroad on export business for more than thirty days in a tax year were given tax-free benefits relating to the time away. David's tax bill reduced quite significantly, making meeting school fees a good deal easier.

It was with Thatcher's support in 1982 that the British company, Northern Engineering Industries Ltd (NEI), was awarded the design and construction management contract for the Rihand 2000MW coal-fired power station in India. Lin Ollier met the NEI directors at the World Energy Congress in India in 1978 and this led to Allott & Lomax being retained for the civil/structural and architectural design of the power station.

Roger Hyde was to be the director responsible for the Rihand project. However, he fell ill on his first visit to India and it was decided David should take over. For some years now, David had been focusing on overseas work and not involved in power station work. He needed to quickly get up to speed with how the power industry had moved on in the meantime. He took himself off, with Helga, to attend the North American Power Conference in Toronto and was soon back in the groove again.

57. Rihand Power Station, India

58. Rihand cooling water tunnel

However, turning the UK economy round proved to be a slow process for the Thatcher government. Interest rates at 17% and an overvalued pound led to a dramatic collapse of much of the UK industrial base and high unemployment.

Fortunately, Allotts at this time were also engaged in the design of the massive nuclear fuel thermal oxide reprocessing plant for British Nuclear Fuels at Sellafield, known as THORP. The small architectural section in David's department was transferred to his co-director, Les Lee's team on THORP. During this work, the Allott architectural design team became the second largest architectural office in the UK, with the pure architectural practices in the country struggling for work.

Thatcher's ratings slipped and the horror of returning to a Labour government loomed. Then Argentina invaded the Falklands in 1982. Thatcher did not hesitate and the rest is history with the Falklands retaken within months. Thatcher's ratings shot up, as did the prestige of the UK.

North Sea oil production was now more than two million barrels per day. Even the Arabs were beginning to respect the UK again.

Allotts had now joined their London competitors as a leading international consulting engineer and David's hope to see the world through his work had become a reality.

By 1982, Roger Boissier had become involved in Allott & Lomax. He had worked on the same power station site as Roger Hyde in their early careers. Roger Boissier was a non-executive director of a number of large companies, including British Gas and Severn Trent Water as well as being chairman of Royal Crown Derby. He was a networker par excellence, and being a member of the World Energy Congress British Committee, he was well known throughout the industry at home and abroad.

It is true to say that David was uneasy about the involvement of Roger Boissier, 'Roger B', as he was to become known in Allotts. Was he being lined up to become chairman of Allott & Lomax? A job David had his eye on!

However, when they first met, it turned out they had much in common with Roger being the brother-in-law of Lord Lonsdale, whom David knew well having been the tenant of Whale Moor Bothy on Lord Lonsdale's estate. Roger was to prove an important part of David's team in the years ahead.

Networking plays a significant part in business. Formal gatherings at industry dinners and conferences provide the environment for networking with business leaders exchanging ideas and launching new ones. At this time, few wives of business leaders went out to work. Wives attended such events and played a vital role in creating a relaxed atmosphere amongst delegates enabling the further strengthening of business ties and the opportunity to create new ones. Lin Ollier realised that amongst 'Allott wives', it was Helga who had the qualities to play a lead role on behalf of the company on such occasions and it became a significant part of her life until David retired. Roger Boissier's wife, Bridget, worked with Helga in this capacity.

Helga's role in support of Allott & Lomax took a significant step forward in 1982 when she was a member of the Allott & Lomax delegation to the World Energy Congress in Cannes in the South of France. David and Helga were the junior members of the Allott delegation, there to help host two Allott lunches for clients and potential clients and then to return to England before the end of the conference.

Conscious of their junior position in the Allott delegation, they naturally held back at the check in at the Carlton Intercontinental Hotel to let their seniors check in and be taken to their rooms. Fortunately, this had taken place by the time David and Helga moved up to the check-in desk.

They were received by a broad smile from the receptionist. "How pleased we are to welcome you to our hotel, Mr and Mrs Compston. We have upgraded you to a large room with a view of the sea," David always stayed at Intercontinental Hotels on his business travels round the world and held their 'loyalty card'. David and Helga made sure that the rest of the Allott delegation were unaware of the special treatment they were having at the Carlton, it would not do for the junior members of the delegation to have the best room!

Roger Boissier, being part of the Allott delegation, had arranged that the Allott lunches should be something special and different to the usual corporate functions hosted by companies in the big hotels. A restaurant in the charming village of Mougins was chosen. The tables were set outside looking across the village square. The restaurant had established itself as the first in the world to offer nouvelle cuisine.

Each of the Allott delegation hosted a table of guests; the 'great and the good' of the world energy

59. Helga with Allot lunch Guests at World Energy Congress in Cannes

scene. This was quite daunting for David, never mind Helga. However, she did her stuff on this first such occasion, many more were to follow.

In 1984, David persuaded his co-directors that the time had come for Allott & Lomax to embrace the American approach to obtaining new business. This was accepted even though it infringed the rules of professional conduct of the Association of Consulting Engineers, of which all Allotts directors were still members.

A sales and marketing department was established under David's direction and managed by Will Paskins. It was becoming very clear that Allotts reliance for business on the UK power and nuclear sectors was not a sound strategy for the future. Consequently, a very major market research exercise was undertaken with the objective of identifying the future for the company.

This led to a strategy to maintain strength in the power and nuclear sectors as the 'backbone' of the business, while achieving a balance in turnover by increasing the volume of work in other sectors in which the company had a small foothold and entering new markets. The market research had identified two new sectors which provided the prospect of significant future business.

The first was leisure which was seen as an expanding part of life's balance in the UK as the standard of living improved. Now, the theme park industry was looking to create new and ever more exciting experiences with rides becoming more and more outrageous and frightening and people liked this! However, the engineering of these rides was very sophisticated and safety standards in design and operation clearly were a matter of the greatest importance to the theme park owners. They did not have the engineering skills to ensure safety. Allotts realised they could sell their safety culture, well-embedded in the company from their long standing involvement in the nuclear industry, to the theme park industry.

A chance meeting on holiday abroad of an Allott director with a director of Blackpool Pleasure Beach, the UK's largest theme park, led to the topic of safety on rides and that the Blackpool company was looking for an independent engineer to carry out checks on their rides.

John Roberts was quickly dispatched to meet the owners of Blackpool Pleasure Beach and was invited by them to submit proposals to act as their consulting engineers on rides. John was successful in persuading them that Allotts was the company for the job. He then secured similar commissions for Alton Towers and Chessington World of Adventure. In 1991, Blackpool Pleasure Beach launched their next major project, the construction of the world's second largest rollercoaster to become known as Pepsi Max The Big One (later called just The Big One) and on which Allotts acted as the owner's engineer. John has been their consultant ever since. Allotts practically swept the market as the UK's theme park consulting engineers, designing a timber roller coaster for Gulliver's World and going on to work at the Universal Studios 'Island of Adventure' in Florida with other overseas work in France, Spain and Norway.

60. 'Pepsi Max' – The Big One

Such was the reputation which John quickly achieved that when Disney decided to build their Paris Disneyland, their rides design team came to Allotts offices in Sale. Announcing themselves as "Imagineers," Allotts gave them a presentation of Allotts work on UK theme parks in the hope of obtaining some of the work for the Paris project.

However, it became clear that the American imagineers were very competent professional engineers, they having designed all the American Disney rides 'in house', and they would be designing the rides for Paris Disneyland. During the next two days, the American party planned to visit Blackpool Pleasure Beach and Alton Towers theme park, both Allott clients. Surprisingly, they had not arranged to meet the operators at either place.

John said he would contact Mr Thompson at Blackpool to make sure the most benefit could be achieved by Disney from their visit but, at the same time, explaining that the Blackpool site would perhaps seem small compared with Disneyland in California. However, the leader of the American party said that they wanted to see Blackpool Pleasure Beach as it was the site of the most rides in one place in the world, more than they had in Disneyland.

The Thompsons responded at once and invited David and John to bring the Americans for lunch the next day in the tower restaurant at the Blackpool Pleasure Beach. Arriving in time for a pre-lunch drinks reception, hosted by Mr and Mrs Thompson overlooking all the rides the Americans had come to see, as lunch was announced, the lift door opened and at that moment Mrs Thompson senior, the matriarch of the family and founder of the company with her husband, invited all to sit down for the meal. This sure was showmanship, but then the Thompsons were showmen par excellence.

Allotts' handling of the opportunity to enter the theme park industry demonstrated a complete cultural change within the business, with Allotts leading the way into the future of the marketing of professional services in the UK.

The Confederation of British Industries acknowledged Allotts' achievements in this respect in an article published in the CBI News of July 1986 stating, "In doing so, the company (Allott & Lomax) has adopted modern marketing techniques more familiar to the world of multinationals than to a professional engineering consultancy."

The other new market Allotts had identified was defence. Unlike leisure, this could not be entered just with a bit of luck. Operated by the civil service in the Ministry of Defence, the challenge was for Allotts to understand the system and procedures leading to being included in tender lists. Allotts joined the Defence Manufacturers' Association, with John Mills representing the company at their meetings, thereby learning about government procurement.

Managing for success

Since 1981, Allott & Lomax, a Manchester-based firm of consulting engineers, has expanded into new international markets and trebled its staff. Its approach to spotting market opportunities shows how a firm can exploit new business techniques and adapt them to the needs of highly competitive world markets...

Allott & Lomax is a major force in power station design in the UK and in Latin America. Its work involves the planning and design of capital projects worth hundreds of millions of pounds. At a time of booming world growth in the 1960s with energy consumption escalating, the company's fortunes, founded largely on oil and coal fired power station construction, seemed assured. However, conscious of the dangers of overdependence on a single sector, the company sought out and developed new markets in the Middle East and West Africa. Diversification was given further impetus by the oil price shock of 1972; this led the company to explore entirely new markets.

Like many British companies, Allott & Lomax's approach to market development had, until the early 1980s, been based on the considerable experience of the Board rather than on a more rigorous statistical approach. During the mid-1970s the company undertook limited market research which identified the rapidly emerging nuclear fuel industry as a key opening for the company's services. The Board were impressed by the effectiveness of this market research exercise which enabled the Company to exploit a profitable and developing market.

World recession, diminishing prospects within the oil-rich states and a reduction in investment in new nuclear fuel processing plant necessitated a major strategic rethink in the late 1970s. Drawing on lessons learned during research into the opportunities within the nuclear industry, chief executive Roger Hyde turned to the substantial in-house

A new series complementing 'British Success', Managing for Success will be looking in more depth at how successful companies have managed to become world beaters.

expertise developed via industrial feasibility studies conducted in the last decade. Doubts remained: Could a team with little experience of the company's mainstream activities get to grips with the complexities of the international engineering business? And could they equal the Boards' extensive and diverse knowledge of the business?

To overcome these hurdles the research team examined a sector in which the company is predominant (power station construction) and

ALLOTT & LOMAX

ducted their research without reference to the Directors' personal knowledge. The first report took some four months to produce and quickly established the team's competence in the Board's eyes. Its conclusions coincided almost perfectly with the Director's views on the power station market: yet it did so with a thorough statistical and sectoral analysis which emphasised the experience and intuition of Board members to be quantified and decision making to be speeded up.

The company's market research initiative epitomizes the successful partnership of industry and academia which characterises much of the nation's best industrial endeavour. The company's inhouse team of a business studies graduate supported by two undergraduates on industrial placement was supplemented with expertise from the marketing departments at Salford University and North Staffordshire Polytechnic. Principal lecturer Les Trustrum comments that the project has been of considerable benefit to all involved; the company has gained valuable market intelligence, the staff received in-career training and the academics front-line industrial experience to take

back to the lecture theatre.

The result has been the development of a unique computerised database for evolving detailed, qualitative forecasts of capital expenditure by the construction sector for both the UK and developing countries. The majority of the research has been based on exhaustive data searches, analysed with typical engineering practicality.

The company has ranged far and wide in its search for relevant data from planning and public enquiry information to government and regional authority publications, government, professional institution and trade statistics, EC and aid institution information, articles from newspapers and journals, bank reports, annual reports, books and other published surveys. Steps are now being taken to ensure the initial market data base is regularly reviewed and kept up to date, whilst embarking on further, more detailed market research.

The impact of this exercise, costing less than ½% of turnover has been dramatic, allowing the firm to embark on a new rationalised approach aimed at enhancing

ALLOTT & LOMAX

performance. In particular, the need, location and activities of its UK regional offices has been reviewed with emphasis being placed on the 'ambassadorial' role of a new London office. The function of its overseas offices have been rationalised while maintaining a commitment to overseas work from a strengthened and re-organised UK headquarters. A sophisticated financial management system has been introduced resulting from an awareness to optimise the size of the firm and minimise overheads while maintaining the

highest standards of service.

Whatever changes markets throw up in the next decade, Allott & Lomax plans to be one step ahead. If its past performance is anything to go on, it is likely to succeed.

The lessons:

● Complacency is the enemy of business success. An ability to look beyond the immediate day-to-day concerns of the company and adopt a strategic view is a key determinant of long-term prosperity. The marketing initiative has enabled Allott & Lomax to anticipate changes in demand rather than react to them. In doing so, the company has adopted modern marketing techniques more familiar to the world of multinationals than to a professional engineering consultancy. It has also been able to diversify as Allott & Lomax now provides business development services through its new subsidiary, Allott & Lomax (Industrial Consultants) Ltd.

● Universities represent an under-utilised source of low cost, high quality expertise. Allott & Lomax successfully launched a highly involved market research exercise drawing heavily on expertise from a local university and polytechnic. Industry Year is all about building bridges between education and industry. The company's experience shows how very fruitful such links can be.

● The research team's pilot study of power station construction shows an appreciation of the importance of winning support *within* the company for new ideas. If a concept is sound it can often be proved to everyone in the company before its launch. The team at Allott & Lomax gained the confidence and support of the Board with their first report – this ensured both that the company put its full weight behind the market research initiative and that the team's conclusions were fully implemented. The benefits were almost immediate.

● If you would like to contribute to Managing for Success, please contact Ian Stewart (ext 2408).

61. CBI News – Managing for success

155

With the backing of the Allotts' sales and marketing department, John succeeded in Allotts being included on the MoD list of approved contractors.

This milestone achieved, the company began to win contracts regularly for the design and construction supervision of new facilities for the army and RAF.

David and Helga had moved from Stonegate Cottage to Aberfells near Kirkoswald in Cumbria in 1982, giving up Whale Moor Bothy and buying a small flat in Knutsford as a place to stay near the office in Sale when necessary.

Helga became very involved in charity work in Cumbria. She was part of the Penrith Meals on Wheels group delivering hot meals to old people, also on the North Cumbria RNLI committee, the local Red Cross group and the Westmoreland MENCAP committee. She served on the local branch committee of the Penrith and Border Conservative Association and was an active member of the Cumbrian Women's Institute.

In 1984, a year after Thatcher's landslide election victory, the miners had turned to strike tactics again. This time the government was prepared. Thatcher had shuffled her cabinet ministers to have those she needed in the right positions to advise and support her in anticipation of the trouble to come. She had even arranged for the appointment of new chairmen to head up the National Coal Board (NCB) and the Central Electricity Generating Board (CEGB). With these changes in place, the electricity generating industry had been put on a war footing. All power stations had to hold stocks of coal that would last longer than it was calculated the miners could last on strike. The power stations even had to have in place their stores of consumables from industrial gasses to lubrication oils and even chemicals for the laboratories to outlast the miners' strike and be unaffected by pickets at the gate. The strike resulted in ugly riots but the rest is history. The miners were beaten by the spring of 1985 and the trade unions never again held power over the government.

Thatcher could now turn her full attention to putting her vision of the UK into practice, a vision that involved a shake-up of the structure of industries and the professions, and a return to a strong work ethic.

By the time Lin Ollier retired in 1987, Allotts had become an international company. Through the takeover of the Birmingham-based consulting engineers, Sir Herbert Humphries and McDonald, there were now mechanical and electrical services engineering expertise to add to Allotts' skills. The group had offices in the Middle East, Nigeria and Germany, in addition to England and Scotland. In the previous ten years, work had been undertaken in thirty-six countries across the world.

Although Allotts operated as a limited liability company, its financial structure was that of a private partnership. The equity was entirely held by the directors, with the shareholdings being distributed from the largest tranche being held by the most senior director with there being a decreasing holding from director to director based on time served on the board to the last appointed director having the smallest holding. There was no bank or other outside holding of equity in the company. When directors retired, they took their financial stake with them.

When Lin Ollier retired, Roger Hyde became chairman for a brief period of less than two years before David became chairman in 1989. In the period leading up to 1989, six of the shareholding directors had retired in quick succession. Consequently, there had been a very significant withdrawal of capital from the company when David took over the leadership. This was to provide a difficult background to David's chairmanship. Furthermore, Thatcher's policies of changes, which were to impact on the business environment, were now being introduced to provide another major challenge for Allotts.

Lin Ollier offered David a piece of advice. He told him that Roger had told him that he, Lin, made the mistake of giving up specific responsibility as director in charge of a project when he became chairman. David responded that Lin had certainly not made that mistake, as chairman one was responsible for all projects and everything else the business was doing. Lin got it right and David would follow his example. In fact, soon after Roger Hyde took over as chairman, David was approached at an energy industry dinner in London by the chairman and chief executive of Northern Ireland Electricity to explain to Roger that they felt he should give up the responsibility for their Kilroot power station project in view of his responsibilities running the company. Helga remembers well David returning to their table to say NEI had given him a rather delicate job to do!

CHAPTER THIRTEEN
Now This Means Business

Mrs Thatcher had been prime minister for ten years when David became chairman of the Allott & Lomax group of companies in 1989. Her impact on business was to be dramatic and long-lasting. Britain was well known for its class system, broadly the landed gentry (the upper class), the professional class and trade (the middle classes) and the working class (the lower class). Thatcher's parents were in trade having a shop in Lincolnshire. On reflection, it seems her parents' background had quite an influence on Margaret Thatcher, when prime minister.

Politicians over the years had had a good go at the landed gentry using the tax system to 'bring them down to earth.' Some had been hard hit but many were up for the fight and continued to prosper. Thatcher now had the professions in her sights. With some justification, she objected to their restrictive practices and aimed to expose them to the full force of the free and competitive market. She acted to achieve this. First, she focused on practices in the stock exchange, resulting in the removal of restrictive practices in 1986 being referred to as the financial markets' 'Big Bang'. Restrictive practices in other professions, including lawyers, architects and engineers, were not going to be tolerated.

Certainly, these objectives had their merits but like all revolutionary changes they had their downsides. In time, many in the professions lost their overriding ethical culture where serving the client came before profit. Lawyers resorted to chasing business on 'a no win, no fee' basis encouraging the public to try to claim off someone regardless of the trouble they were in due to their own carelessness or stupidity. Bankers became so untrustworthy that, to generate bonuses for themselves, they even fiddled international exchange rates and sold services to customers who did not realise they did not need them or even know they were being charged. For some medics, a five day week was being put before attending the patient.

The construction sector professions were impacted by Thatcher's view that fixed price design and build contracts, known as 'turnkey', were the way ahead. To her, this would avoid cost and time overruns. With government contracts increasingly awarded on this basis, the same approach was taken up by the private sector.

While fixed price design and build could be beneficial for projects which were not too complicated, it is a different matter for the large complex projects. Such a system requires each contactor tendering to involve a design and quantity surveying team to produce their proposal and cost it. This is clearly an extra overhead which can only be recovered through those contracts that are won and must therefore be spread across the overhead element of every tender. Furthermore, there is also a higher risk element to be added to the price. The alternative is for the project owner to involve one design and quantity surveying team to fully detail the tender drawings, specifications and bills of quantities, which are then used as the basis of the tenders received from contractors. This latter approach removes much of the risk for contractors and saves a significant cost when preparing tenders.

Thatcher also achieved her objective of the privatisation of more than fifty public undertakings. It had been 'a marathon' taking place over many years and included gas, water and electricity, the latter being in process of privatisation when she was forced from office in 1990. Her aim was to encourage the public in share ownership in revitalised efficient companies. With the privatisation of electricity, gas and water the hope was also for a resultant reduction in charges.

Before privatisation of the electricity industry, the Central Electricity Generating Board (CEGB) employed a small planning team that forecast future demand and planned the required investment in new power stations and the distribution system, with the Scottish and Northern Ireland utilities doing the same. Care was taken to arrange for there to be a diversification of types of generating plant between different fossil fuels, nuclear and hydro. The utilities were big enough with government backing to undertake the major projects involved. They compared their charges with those made by the other major utilities including Electricity de France and the USA's largest electricity utilities, to ensure they were competitive and fair. The plans put in place by the UK's nationalised utilities from the mid 1950s served the nation well for over sixty years.

At the time of writing in 2015, the privatised electricity industry was based on the 'Big Six' companies which generated and distributed electricity, with several more companies supplying electricity even though most had practically no generating capacity! This group even included the Co-op! Since privatisation, politicians had become involved in interminable debate about the future of the industry, with the result that no decisions had been taken at the appropriate time for the necessary replacement of ageing generating capacity.

Worst still, none of the so-called 'Big Six' was big enough to undertake the risk of the investment required. Even more distressing for those who had played their part in the past designing and building power stations which were constructed and installed with plant entirely of British manufacture, was that the Chinese would be involved in the next programme of construction of new power stations, since the great British manufacturers which had supplied the industry and the world were no more.

Even Thatcher's vision of the British public holding shares in the utilities had been compromised by the fact that some of the 'Big Six' were by now owned by European utilities.

Politicians also became so deeply involved in the proposals for transportation and infrastructure projects, relying on the hope that contractors would undoubtedly take a good deal of the risk, with the result that, as in the power industry, decisions were forever being postponed, be it for vital airport expansion or upgrading of the rail network to match the European high-speed system.

Meanwhile, back in 1989, it was David's job to ensure Allotts adjusted to the business environment which was the legacy of the Thatcher government. 'Change' became the 'in' word in business. Allotts had to change and change quickly. The business had to become very commercially astute while maintaining its professional services to the highest standards on which its reputation and future depended. It was important there was strict management control of cost and quality of services. This required rationalisation of the management structure supported by a state of the art IT management information system. This was developed in-house by Will Paskins, now a director, who had set up the much-praised marketing techniques adopted by the company a few years earlier. A distinguished corporate style was also developed in-house and adopted throughout the Allott Group. A London office had been opened with a prestigious address in Buckingham Gate. Instead of being involved with the Association of Consulting Engineers, David became active in the Confederation of British Industries, the

CBI.

With David taking over as chairman of Allotts, it was time for a change of home as well; to be within a daily commute of Allotts headquarters in Sale near Manchester. Until now, David and Helga had always had a home or 'bolt-hole' in their beloved north Cumbria. Helga had become very active in supporting charities and the Conservative Party in north Cumbria, David had his salmon fishing on the River Derwent for the past forty years and they both loved fell walking. They had a wide circle of friends in the area. They wanted to remain close to their friends and interests, to still be in Cumbria while in easy reach of Sale. After several months of search, they bought Parsons Hill in Barbon near Kirkby Lonsdale, Barbon being beautifully situated in the centre of 'Ruskin's View' from the churchyard in Kirkby Lonsdale being the subject of the famous painting by J. M. W. Turner.

6. J.W.M. Turner's Ruskin's View

By now, Allotts was established as a defence contractor. Then the Allott reputation in nuclear civil/structural engineering and architecture was to play a key part in the company being shortlisted to tender for the role of nuclear works adviser for the upgrading of the Royal Naval dockyard in Plymouth, which was to provide refit facilities for the navy's nuclear submarine fleet. This would be a very major contract.

Finally, just two companies remained in the running for the contract, Allotts and the UK's largest manufacturer. Alan Smith led the Allott team for the final interview in Plymouth with the Ministry of Defence (MoD), being the director nominated who would be resident in Plymouth if the contract was won. It was a very long and tough interview lasting several hours with a break in the middle. Alan rang David during the break to say it was very hard going and he was not too hopeful of the outcome. David said he considered the MoD were making sure he was man enough for the vital task of leading the nuclear works' adviser team. Alan returned to the second half of the interview to prove he had what it would take, and he did so. This very important contract was won and ran for many years. A wide range of more work from the Ministry of Defence in England and Germany was secured over the years ahead.

At the same time, under Ed Hill's direction, Allotts expanded their mechanical and electrical services business mainly based in Reading, where Steve Sellwood was in charge. Work secured included the upgrading of the mechanical and electrical services of the Kensington London Hilton and for the US Air Force bases in Eastern England, as well as involvement in numerous Somerfield supermarket projects.

Under Dieter Deffner's management, Inkolpan in Germany was quick to take advantage of the reunification of the country, opening offices in the former East Germany, and obtaining German aid-funded work supporting German ethnic population in the former USSR. Inkoplan undertook the design of the underground services for the new Athens International Airport.

In October 1992 Inkoplan with Allott & Lomax took part in a British companies' exhibition in Leipzig in former East Germany on the occasion of the Queen's historic visit to Dresden. She then travelled to the Leipzig exhibition in the afternoon, Helga receiving the Duke of Edinburgh while David was introduced to the Queen.

Most people meeting the Queen for the first time are a little nervous and concerned as to what to talk about. David was no exception. However, the Queen is always so well briefed about the people she is to meet and at once opens the conversation.

63. Inkoplan mobile office in former USS with Dieter Deffner (left)

She asked David if Inkoplan had any work near Leipzig. David was able to explain the company was currently involved in the road improvements near Leipzig Airport and trusted she and the Duke, having just passed through there, were not held up.

Maintaining that strong workload in power and civil nuclear work had to be achieved against the background of the changes in the industry introduced by the Thatcher government. No longer did the work 'come through the front door' from the long-established client, CEGB. It no longer existed. Now, there were the new power utilities established in the private sector. They were looking to place contracts on a design and build basis for their expansion of generating capacity based gas turbine machinery. The Allott power sector marketing strategy relied quite significantly on the networking done against the background of involvement in the World Energy Congress (WEC) with its meetings at three-yearly intervals.

64. David and Hlga meet the Queen in Liepzig

Following the success of the 'Allott Lunches' at the WEC in Cannes, it was decided Allott Lunches would be arranged at the future World Energy Congresses. The challenge was to match the venue and quality of food in Cannes. Helga played a key role as host, with Roger Boissier, David and other directors involved in the power sector work in support at the lunches.

In 1986, the congress was held in Montreal. An ideal venue was chosen being run by friends of those who owned the restaurant in Mougins, where Allotts held their lunches at the WEC in Cannes. Then, just months before the congress was due to start, the restaurant was sold to some Japanese! Panic stations! David set off to find a new venue. He found one with an excellent reputation for French cuisine, although owned by a Polish chef. The lunch was another remarkable success. Just before the guests were due to arrive to be received by Helga and David, Helga came to tell David two officers of the Canadian Mounted Police had arrived. Such was the status of the Allott guest list that the lunch had been identified as meriting security cover by the police.

Four years later, the WEC was held in Madrid and then, in 1994, in Tokyo, Japan. It was a real challenge to find a special venue near Tokyo serving the French cuisine for which the Allott Lunches had become so renowned. As ever, Roger Boissier was on hand to help. Roger appreciated the best of cuisine and knew where to find it in London. He approached a friend who was a renowned chef and whose restaurant Roger often patronised. In turn, his friend introduced Roger to Party Planners, a company specialising in organising society and corporate events at home and abroad.

Party Planners had been established by Lady Elizabeth Anson, a cousin of the Queen, and had a partner based in Cheshire, Juliet Maynard. Juliet arranged to meet David in his office. This very attractive and businesslike young lady arrived. She arranged for David to 'try out' two possible restaurants in Tokyo on his forthcoming visit to Japan. Juliet certainly made an impression on David. However, the restaurants were in central Tokyo, difficult to access easily from the venue for the WEC which was located a significant distance outside the city.

However, David had friends who were based in Tokyo at that time. They recommended a restaurant in the country not too far from the WEC venue. It was set in the most charming buildings of an old traditional Japanese farm. A feature was a long dining table cut from the trunk of a huge tree beautifully polished. The restaurant specialised in French cuisine! Again, the lunch was a great success. Associated with the restaurant there was a pottery producing handmade items with a shop which proved to be an extra interest to the ladies after lunch.

By now delegates at the WEC hoped to be included on the 'Allott Lunch' guest list. There could hardly be a better way of promoting the company to the industry. This was to be the last time Helga and David hosted a WEC 'Allott Lunch'. The next WEC would take place days before David was to retire.

Over the years, some quite special thanks were received from guests, none more special than this in verse:

THE ALLOTT & LOMAX LUNCHEON
AN APPRECIATION

With memories fresh, of fun in Spain
in coach we awaited Brits tardy,
But Roger, a gent, expresses no pain
twelve years a co-host – now hardy.

When all aboard 'twas off we went
all expectant Madrid cou'n't be beaton
For 'tis true, Reg and I have often said,
a finer meal we've never eaten.

After miles and miles of cars for sale
It was muttered "the bubble has burst
A&L's lost its way, top Execs brought to play,
Will return still with hunger and thirst"

But in time of short span
we were seated to plan
in this place so carefully selected.
A menu expansive, proved quite a surprise
as more courses arrived than expected

Of course we all knew
the wines'd be true
as those by our hosts' prior tested.
With glee they were flowing
And none felt like going
back to conference now all fed & rested

Words of welcome from David were modest indeed,
given hosting one could not surpass.
But your guests had their say
with thanks for the day,
expressed so well by that man "Bob the gas" *

For Reg Jeune and me 'twas a real luxury
to receive your kind invitation
to this special event, that some may resent
can't include the whole WEC delegation!

Thank you, from Mike & Lesley Liston and
Reg & Monica Jeune
*Sir Robert Evans – Chairman of British Gas

Helga's involvement in the promotion of the firm's business through her key role of host at the World Energy Congresses and other corporate functions in the UK and overseas cannot be overstated. She became a very well-known and -liked figure in the power industry. To this, she added her involvement in the Allott social events throughout the year and particularly leading up to Christmas, attending the firm's office Christmas parties from Devon to London, the Midlands, East Anglia, to Manchester, helping David to build a 'family' team spirit within the company. She did all this while increasingly supporting both her and David's ageing mothers while continuing to be active in charities and local politics.

Work on the mega THORP nuclear reprocessing plant in Cumbria for British Nuclear Fuels had come to an end in 1989. This had involved a large number of Allott staff for several years. The next mega civil nuclear project was to be the Underground Nuclear Waste Repository to also be in Cumbria. The government-owned company UK NIREX Ltd was to be responsible for this project. The scheme involved a £1.25 billion tunnelling complex reaching deep down into the underlying igneous rock. Tenders were due to be issued for the lead design consultant just at the time the Channel Tunnel had been completed. Allotts had almost continuous involvement in the West Cumbrian nuclear site since the outset of the nuclear industry in 1953. However, the company's experience in tunnelling was very limited. The initial challenge was therefore to convince UK NIREX that Allotts merited being included on the tender list.

Heitkamp, Allotts partner in the ownership of Inkoplan in Germany, were, however, a very experienced tunnelling company, including extensive work for the German coal mining industry. Allotts were given the opportunity to make a submission to NIREX, teaming up with Heikamp, to be considered for the tender list. As a result, they were invited to bid against competition which included the Channel Tunnel consulting engineers. It could be said that it was against the odds that Allotts' tender was judged to be the favoured bid. However, before awarding the contract, the chairman of NIREX, Sir Richard Morris, wanted to be satisfied that the Allott/ Heitkamp partnership was a strong one and asked to visit projects in progress involving the companies.

Accordingly, David arranged to accompany Sir Richard to two appropriate current projects as well as arranging for a visit to the German radioactive waste repository very deep down in the salt mines in northern Germany. It was clearly vital that all went well during the visits.

The first visit was to the Channel Tunnel where the final part of the work involved laying the high-speed rail tracks for which Heitkamp had the contract. They had asked Allotts/Inkoplan to second a site engineer to them who was fluent in English and German to supervise the work on the English half of the Tunnel. The tracks were now in place right through the two parallel tunnels with the site engineer in the process of checking the final lengths of track under the middle of the Channel. Arrangements were made for Sir Richard and David to be transported the nine or so miles to see the work being finally completed. Sir Richard had just been briefed on the Heitkamp/Allott/Inkoplan teamwork and the details of what had been involved to meet the high specification for the tracks, when the fire alarm was sounded! Emergency procedures were acted upon at once involving quickly going into the small service tunnel constructed between the two main tunnels. Clearly, neither Heitkamp nor Allotts/Inkoplan had caused the issue resulting in the alarm. However, the thought that Sir Richard, who was of advanced years, might have to walk back nine miles to the Tunnel entrance did not augur well for a successful visit! Fortunately, after some time, a message was received that the emergency was over and had not been caused by fire but a build-up of high carbon gas levels.

In Germany, a very interesting day was had visiting the radioactive waste repository deep in the salt mine. This involved travelling in what was an open-top bus through the network tunnels cut in the salt.

The next day was the visit to the tunnel being constructed by Heitkamp from an existing pithead to a new coalface which was to be opened. The distance from the bottom of the pithead shaft to where the tunnel face was then being cut was about six miles. Transport was by miners' steel rail cars on the narrow-gauge railway, there being twin tracks. The rail cars were just wide enough for one person to sit facing another opposite, being protected by a steel partition from the next compartment and a steel curved roof but no door. An inspection was made of the work at the tunnel face before boarding the 'train' to head back to the lift to the pithead. After about four miles, an empty train of trucks going to collect more of the excavated material from the tunnel face could be heard coming, making a lot of banging noises. As it passed, it was realised unbeknown to its driver that the last truck had been derailed and was being dragged along. As it reached Sir Richard and David's rail car, it crashed into it and derailed it! Now, the only thing to do was to set off walking the two miles to the lift. After the emergency in the Channel Tunnel, David could not believe that something else had gone wrong on the visits intended to impress Sir Richard! Fortunately, Sir Richard took it all in good part and was satisfied that Allott with Heitkamp support were the right consultants for the design of the NIREX project. Enquiring from NIREX what had made the Allott bid the most attractive, they were informed that, in addition to demonstrating the necessary geotechnical and tunnelling experience, the Allott bid most importantly showed a clear understanding of the needs of the nuclear industry.

German staff joined Allotts' in a special office established near Harwell, the UK nuclear establishment in southern England. The work proceeded until the basic design had been established and planning permission was sought from the Cumbria County Council. The matter was referred to a public enquiry which amongst the very wide range of issues raised, included considering the situation which could exist after the next ice age! Then the government decided to postpone the decision, which had still not been taken in 2015.

With Mike Sargent, the second most senior director, continuing to oversee work in the power sector, Allotts successfully adjusted to the new approach of the power industry with some utilities turning to design and build turnkey contracts. An additional client base was established with two major European plant manufacturers engaging Allotts as civil/ architectural designers on many new gas turbine power stations in the UK and abroad.

Under the direction of Andrew Ogden, the company expanded its involvement in highways and transportation including moving into rail. Important work included the study to upgrade the East Coast Main Line between London and Scotland for direct services via the Channel Tunnel to Europe.

Throughout this period of business diversification, the whole approach to design procedures was being revolutionised with all staff now using computers for design calculations and drawings being computer generated. From the recent completion of the design of THORP for British Nuclear Fuels at Sellafield, the largest industrial project at that time in the UK, which had involved all drawings being hand drawn, soon there would be no drawing board to be found in any Allott office. This placed a strain on the financing of the business with year after year investment in IT running at about half a million pounds.

With the business now so diversified technically and geographically, it was essential that the management paid the fullest attention to the company's quality assurance procedures. These required that all design calculations and drawings were checked by a nominated senior person with a signed record of those checks being kept. Letters had to be signed by an authorised manager with the appropriate level of delegated authority or a director. Such was the strength of the system that errors were so infrequent that David could only once recall during all the time he worked for the company, a claim from a client had to be referred to the professional indemnity insurers. Email was just coming into use during David's chairmanship. However, Allotts continued to maintain their strict quality assurance procedures based on 'hard copy'.

Nevertheless, in other business sectors the advance of information technology, IT, was seen as an opportunity to dispense with middle management. Helga observed at this time that the headlong rush to rely on IT would all 'end in tears'. The financial services sector was in the forefront in adopting IT to reduce middle management. In 1995, a twenty-eight-year-old, Nick Leeson, employed by the City's oldest merchant bank, Barings, gambled £827 million of the bank's money to try to increase the profit in trading and his bonus. While it was his job to do this trading to make profit from it for the bank, he was not under more senior middle-management supervision. He was found to be operating secretly and was arrested and found guilty of forgery and cheating. His actions were the direct reason for the bank going into liquidation. Over the years thereafter, many more similar issues occurred in the financial services sector, with the financial crisis of 2008 being founded on banks over reliance on IT rather than a strong human input to management. The Libor rigging scandal following the financial crash of 2008 cost banks billions of pounds and dollars in fines. When eventually, at last in 2015, the first individual staff member of a bank was taken to court for playing a key role in Libor rigging while in his twenties, he admitted to being part of a 'dishonest scheme' to rig financial markets, but blamed a 'no rules' culture at the bank for breaking the law! Helga was right, it was all ending in tears, but sadly, the end seemed not to be in sight!

The term 'cyberspace' was coming into use in the 1990s. Leeson might be judged to be in the forefront in communication through cyberspace, the whole world was soon to follow.

Apart from Helga, as James said, there was another lady in David's life, his personal assistant, Anne Rogers. She was a very intelligent, well educated, loyal person. A chairman does not spend his time behind a desk. Leadership requires face to face contact with staff throughout the company while meeting clients and being involved in professional and industry bodies. However, the chairman through the chairman's office has to be in control of the business situation at all times. This was before the advent of emails and text communication to mobile phones. Anne was the 'anchor' and 'gatekeeper' in the chairman's office, keeping in constant contact with David when away from head office, often by the then new invention, the mobile phone, a brick-like gadget.

She attended board meetings, taking the minutes and eventually, was appointed assistant company secretary. While acting as David's PA, she studied and became a member of the Institute of Chartered Secretaries, a legal qualification in company law. She left Allotts soon after David retired to take up a senior post in the company secretary's department of a major stock exchange-quoted British manufacturer. Sadly, she died at the young age of forty-six.

During the nine years of David's chairmanship, the company had the experience of good and difficult times. At the time of his taking over, the company was running at a loss. To this had to be added the significant erosion of the capital base following the retirement of six shareholding partner directors in a short period before 1989.

The recession of 1992 hit the company hard and it took the first three years of David's chairmanship to return the Allott Group to profit. NatWest, the firm's bankers, were naturally uneasy about the reduction in the equity now supporting the business. Their headquarters had issued instructions to the branches to avoid risk in lending to the construction sector. Allotts were ploughing back any surpluses into investment in IT. Despite significant pressure from the bank, Allotts did not 'go bust', unlike the bank itself which did so in 2008!

David became committed to encouraging staff to improve their qualifications, now including those other than technical staff and in 1998, Allotts became recognised as 'an Investor in People' with David Blunkett, the Secretary of State for Education and Employment, presenting the IIP certificate and plaque to the company in the Sale head office.

David had set himself the task of creating a company operating internationally with a balance of work between the sectors within which it was involved doing business. This balance was achieved. He also felt that he was the custodian of the link that Allotts had going back to the great Victorian age of engineering, to Sir William Fairbairn and the Stephensons. Clearly, he had a responsibility to hand over the company in good shape when he retired, which he always had intended to do on reaching sixty in October 1998.

65. Allot 'Investors in People' Group
with Secretary of State, David Blunkett

In the year before David retired, two young architects, Mark and Julia Barfield, had come up with the outrageous idea of a gigantic Ferris wheel on the south Thames bank opposite the House of Commons. The story of how they promoted this idea to become a reality is now part of the history of London. They had initially teamed up with the consulting engineers, Ove Arup. David said to John Roberts, "You have to be involved in this project or you and Allotts will lose the status as the UK's leading consultants on theme park rides." The project was reorganised under the architects with project managers, Mace, and John securing the contract from British Airways as the owner's engineer, with Allotts having responsibility for completely overseeing and approving the design, manufacturing and erection of what became known as the London Eye.

Most of Allotts' work was done after David retired, however he took much pride in the fact that the contract was secured while he was chairman. The story is told in *REINVENTING THE WHEEL*, a beautifully produced book with Foreword by John Roberts and his colleague, Allan Mann. At the peak of the work, Allotts had as many as forty staff involved on the project. The wheel was raised into position by New Year's Eve 1999 and was a focus of the celebrations ushering in the new millennium. John Roberts went on to act as consulting engineer for many similar projects throughout the world.

66. The London Eye

In the last few years before David retired, he had turned his attention to succession planning. In a privately owned company, as Allotts still was, the options are very limited with the next longest serving director expecting to take over as chairman of the group. This was the case with Alan Smith next in line. David had reorganised the board management structure a few years earlier with he himself remaining as executive chairman of the group and Alan Smith as managing director of Allott & Lomax in the UK, to pave the way for Smith to become chairman of the Allott Group.

Sadly, the Compston/Smith relationship was an uncomfortable one with Smith seemingly reluctant to follow the lead which David, supported by the board, was providing. Perhaps Smith found David's dealings with the bank cavalier

67. James with NATO Bosnia Peace Keeping Force

and his risk taking in business a bit much. It certainly did not help the relationship with the issue of David and Helga's son James being included in a proposed redundancy list on James returning from serving as a volunteer TA officer with the NATO peacekeeping force in Bosnia. This, despite the company's stated policy on a plaque in the reception of supporting staff in the military reserve forces and the importance the Ministry of Defence, now a major Allott client, placed on its defence contractors having this policy actively in place. Fortunately, Anne Rogers was alert to this, bringing it to David's attention.

Will Paskins lost confidence in the future for the company and left. Clearly, this would be a major loss to Smith when he took over.

68. James with Challenger Tank with
NATO Bosnia Peace Keeping Force

The Directors' Report and Financial Statements for year ending 30th April 1998 showed the Allott Group in good financial shape with a very significant reduction in bank borrowings. The order book was strong and when David and Helga toured all the branch offices just before he retired, they found them busy and in good heart. By now, there was not a drawing board in sight anywhere in the company, the computer design age had arrived. Not only had IT revolutionised the office environment, but cyberspace was now full of signals from satellites in space.

Farming had changed dramatically since David and Helga were small children living deep in the countryside during the War years of the 1940s. Then teams of farmworkers worked with horses providing the power from ploughing to harvesting. By now, farmers were using self-drive combined harvesters with 'satnav' which not only harvested the crop, but also recorded the quality, yield and moisture content of the grain as these varied throughout the field.

At the same time, a memory bank was produced to be used by the tractors and other machines using the same global positioning system (GPS) to prepare the field for the next crop with fertilisers targeted precisely and being able to work late in the shorter days of autumn and winter.

69. Self-Drive GPS Controlled Combined Harvester

Within twenty years, the self-drive car was being launched. It might be good in the routine urban commute, but one hesitates to think of the car driving itself over Kirkstone Pass in Cumbria!

Retiring as planned at the end of October 1998, David avoided any further involvement in Allotts, taking the view that a 'clear space' should be left for Smith and his board to drive the company forward.

Allotts was due in 2000 to celebrate the 125th anniversary of its founding. Sadly, this special occasion was not to be. Within a brief time of David leaving, Helga heard rumours that merger discussions were taking place with Babtie, consulting engineers of Glasgow. Then, in less than two years Allotts was reported to have become Babtie Allott & Lomax. A few years later, the Allott name was dropped when the Babtie Group was bought by Jacobs

Engineering, a very large American company, which continued to run an office in Manchester, following on with the type of work which had been the 'food and drink' of Allotts business for more than one hundred years.

James had been headhunted by Price Waterhouse Cooper, PWC, the international accountants and consultants, in 2000, initially being involved in marketing the company's services. However, he moved on to joining the consultancy part of the practice, being responsible for the provision of management services for clients in the oil and gas industries, particularly BP, following their Texas City Refinery fire and the Deepwater Horizon Macondo blowout and oil rig fire which resulted in the major oil spill in the Gulf of Mexico. In 2013, he was appointed senior vice-president in SNC Lavalin, the major Canadian oil services and utilities management company. The company holds the technology for the Canadian-designed Candu nuclear reactor. In 2015, James was leading in preliminary discussions with the British government on a proposal for Candu-based nuclear stations to be built possibly at one or more of three sites in the UK, one being Heysham, where his father had originally been responsible for the site feasibility study fifty years earlier.

In 2017, James was closely involved in SNC Lavalin's take-over of the leading UK consulting engineers, W. S. Atkins, then, he being appointed by Lavalin as a non-executive director of Atkins. During David's chairmanship of Allotts, Atkins had been their major competitor. How 'the wheel turns!'

70. James (right) at Number 10

CHAPTER FOURTEEN
The Renaissance of Manchester – A Chance to Give Something Back

With the decline of UK manufacturing in the 1960s, Manchester, like the other major cities in the North and Midlands declined. Facing a very uncertain future, Manchester was in a sorry state. Two things helped Manchester to keep a place on the 'world stage,' Manchester United and *CORONATION STREET*, the TV programme watched worldwide. United were world class and projected the right image for the city. *CORONATION STREET* hardy projected a modern forward-looking city and indeed might be regarded as a fair reflection of Manchester at that time.

Nevertheless, the city council under the leadership of Graham Stringer turned its attention to achieving a brighter future. It was decided to bid as host city for the 1996 Olympic Games. Bob Scott was brought in to lead the bid. However, Manchester was eliminated at the early stages of the bidding process. Undeterred, Manchester bid again for the 2000 Games, coming very close, being second to the winners, Sydney.

Determined to host a multisport international event which would lift the spirit of the city and provide a legacy on which the renaissance of the city could be built, Manchester was successful in being chosen as the host city for the 2002 Commonwealth Games.

Although Allotts had been a Manchester-based business for over a hundred years, apart from being the designers of the several power stations in the region that supplied electricity to the city, the company had had little other work in Manchester. Now a fully diversified construction industry consulting company, it was time to take a share of the developments in Manchester. Firstly, this would involve raising the profile of Allotts and then marketing the wide range of services now offered.

It was against the background of Manchester's determination to reinvent itself as a modern dynamic place which provided an ideal environment for business, living and leisure, that David had the opportunity presented to him to give something back to the city that had provided him with his engineering education and the base from which he had developed a successful career.

The CBI held regular regional group meetings for members to review the current business climate in the area and to provide views of the outlook. This information from all regions formed a background to the CBI's quarterly reports on the economy. David attended these meetings which were also attended by the Bank of England's regional agent. The agent's task is to provide the Bank of England in London with what is going on in business locally and to feed in the views of the business community. This also involved the agent holding one-to-one meetings with certain business leaders judged to have an in-depth view of their particular business sector. David was one of those the Manchester Bank of England agent would meet.

It was at such a meeting David was asked if he would consider being the chairman of the Manchester Training and Enterprise Council. Training and Enterprise Councils (TECs) had been established throughout the country by the Conservative government, being government funded to develop further education, excluding university education, and training aimed at meeting the future needs of business and industry while also encouraging new and expanding businesses.

David was aware of TECs but knew little about them. Nevertheless, he agreed to meet the board members of Manchester TEC. TEC boards were made up of a cross section of people from business, local authorities, further education establishments and the voluntary sector. Board members were unpaid and had to be the head of their organisation, that is chairman or managing directors of businesses, leaders of councils, college heads and the senior manager of a voluntary organisation.

David was invited to be the Manchester TEC chairman in 1992, not long after it had been established. It was a steep learning curve for David, now for the first time in his life working with government and local authorities. It also became clear all too soon that he had been thrown in 'at the deep end.' The TEC board had decided that they wanted the chief executive of the TEC replaced. David made it clear to his board members that he would only act in this regard if and when he had formed his own opinion on the need for a change. The chief executive had been the senior government civil servant in charge of the government office in the north-west before being moved to set up Manchester TEC. Dismissing him from the TEC needed the greatest attention to his rights and a very sound basis for making the change. After sufficient time had passed for David to form his opinion, he had concluded that the chief executive was paying scant attention to the leads the board were duty bound to give. With legal guidance and advice from Roger Boissier, who as a non-executive director of a large public company had had the same task handed to him by the company's merchant bankers, and after having made it clear to the chief executive on a number of occasions that he must pay more attention to the board, David finally told him that, "this is not *YES MINISTER*", the TV comedy show. However, David had also had time to identify a replacement.

The Secretary of State had made it clear that she was very disappointed with Manchester TEC's impact and looked to David to lead the TEC to be recognised as one of the best in the country. To cut a long story short, David, his board and the new chief executive, Richard Guy, set about the challenge which was recognised as having been achieved with David appointed CBE and Richard, OBE, for services to training and enterprise. Needless to say, these honours were a recognition of the Manchester TEC's excellent staff.

David also served on other local bodies involved in Manchester's renaissance as well as serving on the TEC's National Council and being the non-executive member of the Management Board of the Government Offices in the Regions. In all it was like a new career for him, and the perfect antidote for any possible shock from retiring from full-time work!

Graham Stringer sat for Parliament and handed over the leadership of Manchester City Council to Richard Leese in 1996. Richard proved to be an outstandingly successful leader. A man who had the art of delegation and found the right people to work with him; he was enthusiastic about public/private partnership. Although a Labour councillor, he did not have to concern himself with local politics, since he could be confident that Manchester would certainly continue to elect a Labour council. Rather, he turned his attention to bringing about the renaissance of the city. He engaged both the Manchester Training and Enterprise Council and the Manchester Chamber of Commerce and Industry in this endeavour, thus establishing the strongest links with the private sector.

The Commonwealth Games represented the launch of

Manchester back to becoming a world-class destination for inward investment. There was determination that the legacy from the Games would be both a dramatic improvement in facilities for sport and a driver for sustained economic development in the city.

One of the most unexpected and exciting things to happen for David was when he was invited to be a member of the organising committee for the Manchester Commonwealth Games, being appointed a director of Manchester Commonwealth Games Ltd, another steep learning curve!

The Games needed some new major venues, these being the main stadium, the aquatic centre and the velodrome, together with facilities for minor sports. East Manchester was particularly run-down. It was decided the hub of new venues would be there. The exception was the aquatic centre which, with its Olympic-sized competition pool at ground level and a full Olympic-length training pool directly below, located in the centre of the main buildings area of Manchester University. East Manchester became 'Sportcity.' The legacy needs hardy reporting on here. The velodrome became the headquarters of British Cycling. British cyclists became world beaters. Stadia built for major athletics events have little use for such a purpose in the future as many tens of thousands of spectators only attend athletics for Olympics, European Championships and Commonwealth Games; these events moving from city to city over the years. However, an athletics stadium is not ideal for football which does attract large crowds week after week. The Manchester Commonwealth Games stadium was designed to be quickly altered to be an ideal football stadium as soon as the Games were over. The original Games' playing surface was excavated down to the required playing surface for football with additional tiers of seating taken down to be alongside the new pitch. A temporary stand at one end for the Games was replaced with the permanent stand right behind the goal. Manchester City moved in and no longer was in the shadow of Manchester United; City became United's 'noisy neighbours' and Premiership champions.

But Manchester did not want to lose the capacity to host important national athletics meetings in the future. Alongside the main stadium of the Commonwealth Games was the full-sized athletics warm-up track and playing area for field events.

David and other members of the Organising Committee for the Games suggested this facility should be made into an appropriately sized athletics stadium with stands and seating added once the Commonwealth Games were over. With this done, Manchester was now able to host future national athletics meetings.

Inward investment flowed into the city at such a rate that it outpaced even the most optimistic targets set by the council. Richard Leese and the city's chief executive, Howard Bernstein, were both knighted in recognition for the leadership that achieved the renaissance of the city.

70. Manchester Commonwealth Games Directors

71. Manchester Commonwealth Games main stadium

72. Manchester Commonwealth Games

In 2015, Manchester was chosen by the Conservative government to become the first city in the country outside London to be given devolved fiscal powers and be the centre of the Northern Powerhouse in the drive to achieve a balance in the economic environment between north and south.

David considered himself very privileged and fortunate indeed to have been involved in those early days of the renaissance of Manchester. During this time while serving on the various bodies engaged in Manchester's recovery, David steadfastly avoided mixing his business interests with the contacts he had with those responsible for Manchester's development. Nevertheless, the Allott name became well-known to the 'the movers and shakers' in Manchester.

The other directors of Allott & Lomax were not restrained from seeking business in the Manchester region and a 'new local home market' in the Manchester region was established with major roads and bridges projects being secured and significant involvement in the development of Manchester International Airport.

CHAPTER FIFTEEN
At Last, Family Comes First

After returning from his spell in the regular army as a volunteer TA officer in the King's Own Yeomanry with the NATO peacekeeping force in war-torn Bosnia in the early winter of 1996, James met Juliet Maynard, the young lady who had so impressed David when seeking advice on a restaurant in Japan for the Allott Lunch at the World Energy Congress to be held there. In the spring of 1997, James introduced her to his parents and he announced their engagement in April 1998. Very sadly, Juliet's father, Robert, died later that year just before James and Juliet married in January 1999. His family had a traumatic time in World War Two, in sharp contrast to David and Helga.

Robert's mother, Juliet's granny, Ruth Maynard, was born in Darjeeling in India in 1902, being the daughter of a successful German industrialist who became a British national due to his status in India. The family moved back to Hamburg in Germany where Ruth was privately educated. She was one of four children. She married Paul Meyer-Udewald when she was just nineteen years old. They lived in Hamburg and during that time, they had two children, Joan and four years later, Robert.

When the threat of the Third Reich and the anti-Semitic movement made life uncomfortable, they moved to Tilburg in Holland to start a new life, setting up a textile company making linen thread. In 1942, following the German occupation of Holland, the family was detained and taken from their home by train, first to the concentration camp at Vught and then on to Westerbork, where

Ruth was separated from her husband and son. In 1944, the whole family was deported with 900 other people from Westerbork to Bergen-Belsen. However, because of Ruth's British nationality, her family was saved from being sent to Auschwitz. Ruth would have suffered desperate conditions and deprivation. Separated from her husband and son, she was made to work in the camp workshop to be rewarded with tiny amounts of food for her and her daughter.

Miraculously, the family survived Belsen, but as the Germans saw defeat, the family were put on cattle trains without food and sanitation, being shunted back and forth for several days up to the Russian border. Typhus and typhoid broke out on the train from which Ruth's husband and daughter died. When the war ended, Ruth and her son, Robert, who was sixteen years old returned to Tilburg to find all their possessions had been looted and their home was no more. Fortunately, Ruth's mother and sister lived in London and Ruth and Robert moved to start a new life in England, Ruth changing her and Robert's name to Maynard.

Robert went on to establish a company in England involved in the textile industry. His business took him to Northern Ireland where he met and then married Marianne, Juliet's mother.

Robert's death just before James's and Juliet's wedding was a cruel blow to a family who had suffered so much. Nevertheless, Marianne set about organising the wedding and wanted to follow the tradition of the bride's parents arranging and paying for the wedding. She arranged for the reception to be held at Terra Nova School in Jodrell Hall. Unbeknown to her, Jodrell Hall had been the home of Helga's great-uncle, Sir Edwin Stockton. It was an unexpected link at the wedding between the two families.

While work and employment are vital for providing the wherewithal needed for life, it is friends and family that make life worth living.

James's and Juliet's children, George and Hugo, were born in

2001 and 2003. Now, the next chapter in David and Helga's life was to be grandparents. Still living at Barbon in Cumbria, they decided they would move to be near the family, not too near but in easy driving distance, about forty-five minutes away. Their friend, Deiter Deffner, told them if they planned to do this they should do it quickly as grandchildren grow up very quickly! Returning from a holiday with their other great friends, Jim and Gill Kent, on their farm in Cornwall, they called in Shrewsbury and obtained details of The Old Stables in countryside near Oswestry in Shropshire and bought it. It was a forty-minute drive to James and Juliet who now lived in Manley near Chester. Then, very sadly, Juliet's mother died soon after David and Helga moved to Shropshire.

David and Helga soon established a full life in Shropshire, Helga joining the local Women's Institute, David creating a very productive garden for the first time, the climate in Shropshire being more supportive to gardening than in Cumbria. They both joined the National Trust Support Group for Chirk Castle which could be seen in Wales across the Ceiriog Valley from The Old Stables. A little later, Helga joined a branch committee of the League of Friends of the Robert Jones and Agnes Hunt Orthopaedic Hospital, just three miles from The Old Stables, fulfilling her long-term wish to be active in a charity supporting a hospital.

We all have a wide circle of friends, but of those, a few are the special ones.

David and Helga's formative years were spent in remote country agricultural settings. Throughout their life together they found homes in the country. Amongst their closest friends were farmers, Jim and Gill Kent who farmed in Buckinghamshire and the West Country, Sue and Ken Furness, who were nearest neighbours who farmed a field away from Stonegate Cottage in Cheshire and Elizabeth and Robin Raine, who farmed round Aberfells in the Eden Valley in Cumbria. David started holidays with Jim while they were still at school, going to stay with David's Uncle Sandy in Borrowdale in the Lake District. After marrying, they had holidays together with their wives every year from then on. Helga and Sue Furness took their children on holiday each year as they were growing up, Ken being busy at that time of year on the farm. Helga went with Elizabeth to Europe introducing her to overseas travel, before Elizabeth herself became an expert on worldwide travel. When David and Helga moved to Shropshire, Robin and Elizabeth provided David and Helga with a 'bolt-hole' back in Cumbria.

David and Helga were not ones for package holidays, preferring to arrange their own itineraries. It was their two close friends, Dieter in Germany and Sue in California, who took holidays with David and Helga based at Whale Moor Bothy in the Lake District and later in Shropshire on the borders of Wales. Dieter and Sue for their part organising holidays with David and Helga in Germany and California respectively.

2012 was the year of David and Helga's golden wedding, the thirty-first of March being the actual date of the anniversary. They chose to celebrate by inviting all the family and their closest friends who live in England for a weekend at the Howtown Hotel on Ullswater. David had lived in Howtown in the early part of World War Two and it was to Howtown he took Helga on her first visit to the Lake District. The Howtown Hotel has been in the Baldry family for three generations, by now, run by Mrs Baldry and her son, David. Arguably the finest traditional inn in England, it is run deliberately as a 'time warp' of the 1930s, full of antiques, collectables and original paintings. Staff are dressed as in the 30s style, morning tea brought to your room and meals being traditional English cooking, home from home for David and Helga.

Still following the old way of Lakeland hotels closing for the winter season, the Baldrys kindly opened a day early on the Friday before the anniversary date on Saturday. David and Helga with their guests took up the whole of the bedrooms in the hotel with two younger married couples of the family staying in a nearby farmhouse providing them with bed and breakfast while otherwise joining the family at the hotel. The weather was like midsummer, guests arriving on Friday for afternoon cream tea on the lawn and free over the weekend to choose from the very many things one can do in the Lake District. Some went fell walking, James and Juliet took George and Hugo fishing on the lake, others took the steamer to see all of Ullswater and the golfers went off to play at Penrith Golf Club.

As Dieter predicted, George and Hugo grew up quickly, starting school near home and then moving to boarding schools in Shropshire. By chance, David and Helga now found they were living nearer to the boys at school than their parents. The two boys had brought immense pleasure and interest to David and Helga's life, who now could adopt a lifestyle where, 'family comes first.'

73. *Family wedding 2011 BACK ROW: Juliet, David, Helga, James SEATED: Hugo, Stephen (Juliet's brother), Juliana, George*

APPENDIX
ROBERT STOCKTON 'THE WALKER'
November 1889

b May 29, 1821   **d March 1889**

by
His Son Robert Stockton Junior

"Blessed be those how e'er humble, that have their honest wills."
(Shakespeare)

The words of the illustrious poet were never more justly applied than as a tribute to the life of which the following is a memoir. The conscientiousness, combined with a strong sentiment of charity, of which his life was an example, endeared him to all who knew him. Other qualities, not so prominent, but sufficiently conspicuous, will be found portrayed in the following pages, as far as the writer is able to reflect them. Not this latter wishes to convey the idea that his subject is faultless, or even that his opportunities for worldly progress were the most of, but at any rate, that he has left in his large family circle a tender recollection, and has, at the age of sixty-eight, fairly earned the 'well done' of his master at the conclusion of his earth's work.

Robert Stockton was born on the 29th of May, 1821; he was one of the younger sons of Joseph Stockton, of Bunbury, near Tarporley, Cheshire, which latter village was his birthplace. He had six brothers and five sisters, of which he survived all except his eldest brother George, who is at the present time 87 years of age, being born in the year 1802 and who is residing at Burwardsley, still in the enjoyment of good health. Many nephews and nieces, with their children, live in the neighbourhood, or the surrounding villages. The part of Cheshire referred to is one of the most beautiful portions of the county. Words would not convey to the town-dweller, the poetical beauty of nature here presented. The undulating ground rich in foliage, with numerous woods and forest, springs and rivulets, shady lanes, avenues of trees, with the fragrant air and myriads of birds, rich pasture land, yielding farm produce of the best quality, the tidy, well-kept roads and clean cottages studied in picturesque situations, the pretty quaint villages, and above all, the civil country folk of these parts, must be seen and encountered to be a all adequately appreciated. And as the acquaintance with the villages in question is not one of the easiest of matters, seeing that there is only one line of railway which in any way suggests human artifices in this natural grandeur. This is the London & North Western Railway from Crewe to Chester, and the station nearest the village of Bunbury is "Beeston Castle". A good cyclist, or better still, a good pedestrian, has the best facility of exploring such country, and right well is the journey here repaid. The writer, astride a fifty inch driving wheel has enjoyed the view he is attempting to describe, in company generally of his two old friends, Tom Cross and Will Shenton, and the pleasures of his excursions have been enhanced by knowing he was breathing the 'family native air', that he could, so to speak, claim a relationship with the romantic beauties around. About a mile from Bunbury is Beeston Castle, built on a huge rock, and commanding a very extensive view, Liverpool, over twenty miles distant, being plainly visible on clear days, as well as the Estuary of the Dee.

This historical building was erected in 1220 by Ranulph Blunderville, and was for centuries the stronghold of the Earls of Chester. Lord Tollemache is lord of the manor. Beeston is a popular resort for antiquarians. There are numerous legends connected with it, as well as relics of all kinds. There is at the bottom of the well a passage leading to an opening outside the hill at the exterior. There are pictures in the castle by Sir Joshua Reynolds, Gainsborough, Wilson, and Morland. Soon after its erection, the castle was bought by Edward I, when he was determined on the conquest of North Wales, a plan which he successfully carried out. The population is, of course, very sparse, and apart from the gentry, and the nobility, of which there are many ancient families in the neighbourhood, it consists entirely of the agricultural class. At the last census, the village of Bunbury contained about eight hundred and eighty inhabitants, and that of Tarporley about double this number, and it is probable that sixty-eight years ago, that is, the birth of Robert Stockton, the number was not materially different from these figures, taking into account the trifling increase of buildings and the steady influx of villagers into towns and cities. Indeed, we find that as far back as 1227 to 1348, that is, some six hundred years ago, Tarporley possessed a Mayor, and was of some municipal importance, whereas it is now governed by two constables only. This now considered a remote village, would at that period have compared to a place like Manchester, instead of being practically unknown to nine tenths of the people of the latter city as it is now. The Parish Church of Bunbury called St. Boniface, is an old fashioned free stone edifice in the later style of English architecture, with a square tower, surmounted with pinnacles. This church contains several fine monuments, including a rich alter tomb to the memory of Sir Hugh Calverly, a celebrated Cheshire hero, and another to Sir George Beeston. The building was completely restored in 1864. There is a window in the church now containing only a few fragments of old glass which once had upon it an inscription to David of Bunbury. This was the same David to whom Edward I gave a warrant of Protection in the year 1281. Bunbury, though smaller, is probably as ancient as Tarporley. One of the roads leading from it to Acton is called the "Watfield pavement", and as this is also on the line of the South Watling Street from Richborough, in Kent, to Caer Segont, near Carnarvon, and as the similarity between the names 'Whitfield' and 'Watling' is great, there is no doubt that the names of both applied to the same line of way. There is an old college at Bunbury, supposed to have been the residence of priests, and which still contains those characteristics which are common to mansions built in the middle ages. It stands in the north west part of the town.

The appearance of the village is both neat and picturesque.

They speak in raptures of the lands, Beyond the deep blue sea,
But Oh! there is a spot demands,
Much holier love from me, Richest in treasures of the soul,
To comfort man "that's made to mourn",
It is the dearest of them all, The land where I was born.

It will be easily understood that the resourses of a village such as this were limited, and were a great restraint to a large family, almost precluding the possibility of its intactness being preserved. The educational facilities, sixty years ago especially, were of the most meagre kind, reading being principally taught by the aid of the Bible at Sunday School, and any other accomplishment being considered both superfluous and impossible. This, of course, refers to the villages, the gentry received their education, as now, in the great Universities, for public schools even in large cities, were at the time named, few and of a very elementary kind. Nearly all the educational improvements that have been made, have occurred within the last twenty years, that is to say, the changes which were brought about in earlier times have been very slow and timid in comparison with the great strides which have recently been taken. It is only sixteen years since the first London Board School was opened, and it is within the time mentioned that education has become compulsory and, indeed, placed within easy reach of the poorest families.

Printing, sixty years ago was in its young infancy - books of any kind were rare and expensive, indeed it is but seventy-five years since the printing machine was actually invented. Furthermore, steel pens did not come into use until 1832, and for a long time were costly enough, as they were confined practically to one maker, and this Mr. Gillott made a handsome profit by the monopoly. It is necessary to mention these facts, to realise the disadvantage which the family of twelve in question would labour under in this quiet village in the matter of education. Education at that period was strictly confined to the classes, the masses had to be content with either a most primary instruction, or else none whatsoever. In such places it was common, even when schools were ultimately founded, for schoolmasters to ply other avocations, besides teaching, thus a schoolmaster would be also a shoemaker, a tailor would also be a schoolmaster. There are pictures of Webster and Collins which illustrate this. Showing the trifling remuneration attached to teaching in these comparatively modern times, the writer saw quite recently a stone tablet affixed over an old fashioned schoolhouse at Prestbury near Macclesfield, another quaint odd Cheshire village on the following inscription:

"This tablet is affixed in memory of "who gave £100 to be invested by local authorities and the "interest to be paid to a schoolmaster, who shall educate free, "five of the poorest boys of the village. 1793"

This would very likely be considered a liberal, endowment at the time, but our present schoolmasters would look upon this fifteen pence a week as scant pay for the work required to be done. This was in the days when the schoolmaster had his afternoon nap and left his pupils to romp and frolic all over the place meanwhile, the classics, French, Algebra, Etc. were not dreamed of, a little spelling and rudimentary arithmetic was all that was aimed at. It is to be wondered at that Robert Stockton and his eleven brothers and sisters fared badly in the matter of education in their early days? Their father combined shoemaking with farming, sheep shearing, etc. for his and his family's maintenance, and no doubt gave his children whatever facilities in the way of instruction his modest purse would allow. He was often spoken of in terms of admiration by his son Robert, of whom this treats for his many paternal qualities. He was a man of exceptional physique, tall, and well built, but he died about the age of fifty-seven, his wife surviving him many years. The limited resources of employment afforded by the quiet village of Bunbury, coupled with the somewhat premature death of the head of the family, caused most of the children, as they arrived at the age of discretion, to seek their fortunes in other places; some found their way to Chester, others to Manchester; one son ultimately to Bredbury near Stockport, another emigrated to the United States, where he took up the duties of preacher, and it is conjectured that he was the same T.Stockton who was referred to in a sermon by the Rev. Dr. Talmage some two years ago, as a man who was doing good work as an evangelist.

Robert Stockton commenced to contribute to his livelihood at a very early age: he would be no more than ten or eleven years of age when he undertook service at Spurstow Hall, about a mile from his native village. He frequently changed his avocation during the following five or six years. He was an extremely robust youth, and easily able to do farming or other work which came within his sphere. He has told many amusing stories of his early country life. If "small beginnings lead to great endings", his greatness was assured for his beginning was small enough in all conscience. But this short biography is not penned with the object of extolling great deeds, but rather to set off perhaps to a future generation of the family, the admirable disposition and characteristics of their ancestor.

It was quite in 'Dick Whittington' fashion that the object of this history, at the age of seventeen, in the year of the accession of Queen Victoria to the throne, vis. 1838, left his native village for Cottonopolis. There being no railway at the time, except the newly made one from Manchester to Liverpool, and stage coach travelling being expensive, the journey of thirty-five miles was taken on foot, but this was only moderate for the stout healthy limbs which were out on the occasion. It is hardly likely that there was a similar display of grief that our friend Mr. Micawber (of Charles Dickens renown) displayed on his departure from London to Canterbury but rather like the latter evinced on his setting out for the antipodes, for Robert, if leaving brothers and sisters in the lovely heart of Cheshire, was going to join another sister at Irlams O'th Heights, near Manchester, at which latter then considerable town he hoped to find more scope for his natural aptness and ingenuity.

The road through Tarporley to Northwich, twelve miles, is as pretty as the country about Bunbury, already described. It is lined for the most part with fir trees, with considerable woods and clumps here and there, on either side its grassy footpath, and abundance of wild flowers. Nearer, Northwich, long avenues are formed of trees, and this continues in the park like road which leads from the latter town, through Tatton, the seat of Lord Egerton, past Bucklow Hill and Rostherne Mere on the right, Dunham Park on the left to Bowdon. These roads are probably just the same now, as they were in 1838, when they were traversed by the subject of this biography. How many men, who have attained celebrity, have made a beginning in life like this! It is a condition so synonymous with the commencement of a great man's biography, that the author feels tempted even now to pick up his chattels and march on 'somewhere'!

Fortune accompanied Robert on his journey, for before reaching his destination he found temporary employment in the services of a gentleman at Wardle Road, Sale, near Manchester. His sister resided, as already stated at Irlam O'th Heights, which is a hamlet, now considerably grown, about three miles west of Manchester. It appears he had a little difficulty in finding this village (which now more properly describes it) its name and unimportance rendering it unknown to people in the big town, and in answer to his enquiries, he humorously said, he was asked "if it was not somewhere in Ireland"? The sister referred to was Martha, afterwards Mrs. Leigh, somewhat older than himself, and who presently removed to Seedley, to a cottage that stood almost exactly on the site of the Western gateway of the present Seedley Park. The writer recognises a tree in that park now which stood in Mrs. Leigh's garden. She had a considerable family; several of her married daughters reside in and about Manchester now, notably Mrs. Metcalf, at Old Trafford, Mrs. Saville, Weaste, and Mrs.Goodier, at Brooklands. Mrs. Leigh, who suffered for some years from asthma, died about fourteen years ago, soon after her removal from the old cottage in Seedly.

Shortly after his arrival in Irlam O'th Heights, Robert Stockton got employment nearer home. He was for some time at the New Fold Farm, Pendleton, afterwards engaged by Sir Elkanah Armitage, but he was not long with the latter gentleman, for on Sir Elkanah's special recommendation, and an introduction from Sir Robert Peel, he obtained a situation in the Engineer's department of the Lancashire and Yorkshire Railway, under Sir John Hawkshaw, at the offices, Hunt's Bank, Manchester, what is really known now as thePalatine Buildings. But I must go back a little.It was in the hamlet of Irlam O'th Heights he became acquainted with his future wife, Ann, daughter of James Peers of Claremont Road. Here the writer is bound to eulogise: but it is no egotism which prompts him to say that words would really fail to do justice to the mother of the large family which followed this union. Contentment, gentleness, and untiring industry; these are mild terms applied to this estimable parent of thirteen children "laquelle Dieu defend". She is now sixty-four years of age, being born on the 9th of August, 1825, happily in good health. They were married in February 1843, at the 'Old Church', the only name it went by then, now the Manchester Cathedral. It was some dozen years or more later that the Bishopric of Manchester was constituted. Mrs. Stockton's father was a native of Bury. His brother, Edward Peers, attained a high social position there. He was a Manufacturer in the cotton trade, and Edward's son Robert, (cousin to Mrs. S.) resides in that town now, has fully maintained his father's ability and reputation, is an Alderman for the borough, and occupied the Mayoral chair in 1886.

Mr. & Mrs. Stockton first occupied a small house in Sovereign Street, Pendleton, a thoroughfare of old fashioned houses long since demolished. It was there that Edwin was born, on 23rd of September, 1843. Afterwards they lived at the farm New Fold, already spoken of, where a second son Henry, was born on the 2nd of September, 1845. It was at this time, viz. 1845, that his long engagement with the Lancashire & Yorkshire Railway commenced, his connection with such a Company practically forming the focus of this history. He removed his small family from Pendleton to Kent's Place, Ordsall; then to Pleasant Vale, Rochdale Road, and afterwards to Fray's Place, at that time a pleasant little situation on the site of the old fish market, Strangeways, near Victoria Station. Readers who are only familiar with the present aspect of that neighbourhood, will be surprised to hear that these houses looked quite rural; they had long gardens at the front and were in a hollow, and partly secluded from the thoroughfare adjoining.

Before attempting to go into the details with respect to his railway work, perhaps a few remarks as to the standard railways had attained at that time would be useful. It is well known that up to the year 1830 there was not a line of railway in the United Kingdom. The population was much less than at present, and such as it was, was more equally divided between town and country. One effect of railways certainly is to conglomerate the populace into large cities and districts, and to bring about a corresponding diminution of people in rural districts. It is apparent to all that farming as a business, is falling off; not so much because it is not lucrative as for the reason that people will flock together and congregate. Union is strength. There are greater varieties of making a livelihood in large communities than in remote villages. Trade begets trade. Then the pleasures, holidays, cheapness of living, educational privileges, society benefits, are all much greater in large centres than in rural districts. As a consequence of these advantages townspeople are of quicker intellect than their country neighbours, and are looked upon by the latter with awe and mistrust, but sometimes veneration. Up to the time when railways offered their improved mode of travelling, transport both of goods and passengers was effected by stage coaches, country carts, and canal boats. It was a three days' journey and a costly one, from Manchester to London, and people with assets generally made their final depositions before undertaking it. A person who performed the journey was looked up to with admiration as a marvel of experience somewhat in the same light as we should now regard a man who made the journey to Hong Kong. People even well to do lived practically within a radius of twenty miles of their homestead all their lifetime. Newspapers, of which there were but few, cost about 6d a copy; instead of lying about indiscriminately in heaps, they were usually worn to shreds and grew entirely out of date by lending to and fro amongst people who could not afford to buy their own; postage was at about the same rate; a letter, bearing a 6d stamp was an important missive and only written in case of strict need; when Sir Rowland Hill effected the change in 1840 to the modest sum of one penny letters were looked upon by the old generation as trumpery affairs, not worthy of notice, the charm in their idea having rested upon 6d stamp on the cover; bread and flour, for most families baked themselves, was one of the most expensive articles of consumption, a four pound loaf costing two shilling; it was to a great extent debarred from the home of working classes; tea and coffee were luxuries almost unknown, potatoes, buttermilk, oatmeal, home brewed beer etc. being principal articles of diet; the clean pavements and well drained streets and roadways which we are accustomed to in these days, fifty or sixty years ago were muddy, narrow, ill drained, and in a most primitive condition, even in large towns, in London itself: a western town in Ireland would about give one an idea now what the state of things was in England at the time referred to. Moreover, streets were very dimly lighted, Unimportant thoroughfares were not lighted at all except by the little flickering flames in the windows of the inhabitants. Cheap conveyances such as tramcars and omnibuses were quite undreamt of, indeed were not necessary as far a the suburbs were concerned, as such lucky people who could afford to live outside of the bustle of the town, could also indulge in private conveyance. In Manchester, most professional men resided in the very heart of the town; King Street, and St. Anns Square being for a long time considered very desirable quarters for well-to-do people.

To return to the Lancashire & Yorkshire Railway, or, The Manchester and Leeds rail, which it was then. Instead of its present five hundred and fifty miles, its lines at the time referred to were little more than a fifth of that length. The head offices, where Robert Stockton was located, in place of its five hundred clerks comfortably ensconced in spacious, well ventilated rooms, lit by electricity, and with modern conveniences, consisted of a small suite of rooms adjacent to the Palatine Hotel, where, with a mere handful of clerks, and officers, fulfilling plurality of positions, the railway system, such as it was, was managed. It would be impossible to describe the duties of Robert Stockton on his appointment here, in 1845. As far as the writer's knowledge goes, they were those of a semi-clerk and porter, under Mr. Brunlees the Engineer, to whose skill the construction of a considerable part of the L & Y railway is due; it was he, indeed, in conjunction with Mr. Hawkshaw, (afterwards Sir John Hawkshaw) who planned and carried out the gigantic work of making the Summit tunnel, near Todmorden, the only connecting link for a long time of the Lancashire and Yorkshire Sections. Robert established himself with both these, and gentlemen of influence on the Directorate, by his tact and willingness, and was able to survive a sweeping reduction in staff which was made a few years later, a reduction found necessary by the reaction which had set in, in the popularity of railways, and consequent loss of traffic soon after this and a few lines contemporary had been established. Let us try to account for this reaction. There are two parties in the State, the one progressive, the other retrogressive; a change of reform is advocated by the one; it is denounced and opposed by the other; the progressive party has with the aid of education, for nearly a century outnumbered the retrogressive; the reform is at length achieved by the former, whose exertions are no sooner relaxed than the watchfulness and attacks of the latter begin to tell; the result is the "reaction". It has been experienced in all the great advances effected by the progressive party. We have lately seen it on the question of free trade. We have seen the "storm in a teapot" raised by those who would have the struggle fought over again. But we will expound the politics of our subject later.

Victoria Station in 1845 presented a very modest show in comparison with its present aspect. It was little more than half the size it is now. The L. & N.W. Railway had extended the terminus of the old Manchester and Liverpool Road near Knott Mill (where the Offices connected with the original railway still stand) to Victoria, or Hunt's Bank, as the neighbourhood was called, and the L.& Y. Railway simply owned an arrival and a departure platform. The Manchester and Leeds rail was one which quickly followed the Liverpool line. It was incorporated in 1836, partially used a few years later and opened throughout to Normanton in Oct 1st 1844. It was really the commencement of the Lancashire & Yorkshire Railway and it had its terminus and offices at the Potato Wharf, Oldham Road. These offices are still occupied by the L.&Y. Railway Company for the business of the great goods depot which occupies the site, managed by Mr. Jackson, under whom the writer and three of his brothers have at different timed been employed. In the same way that the L.&N. W. Terminus at Liverpool Road was extended, the terminus of the L.&Y. was brought from Oldham Road to Victoria, by the branch at Miles Platting Station, and other lines were soon constructed by separate companies, including the Manchester, Bolton & Bury; the Liverpool and Bury, the Huddersfield & Sheffield, the Wakefield, Pontefract & Goole, the West Riding Union, and the East Lancashire, which gradually immersed into one great system, and formed, in 1847, the Lancashire & Yorkshire Railway (The East Lancashire was not amalgamated until 1859). The extension of the Bolton line from Bailey Street Salford, to Victoria, was effected at a cost of £150,000 being a continuous viaduct, and opened in 1865, the Company having till then used the L.& N.W.L. line between those places. Locomotives and carriages have only assumed their present pretentious and comfortable status after a tedious but steady growth. We are all familiar with the print which represents the first train that ran to Liverpool, with its peculiar shaped engine and open conveyances. Tickets were not required then, the passenger merely paying his fare, for which no receipt was given and walked on to the platform attended by his friends and left the train at his destination without further molestation.

At the time of Robert Stockton's first connection with the L.&Y. Railway of course such things had been improved upon. The locomotives were fairly graceful, their brass facings, now almost abolished, adding much to their appearance. The carriages were for the most part divided into small compartments to hold ten passengers; their seats were upholstered in the first class, the second leathered, the third wooden seats, and not too much in the way of windows, or else entirely open at the sides, each compartment in the latter class being divided by a low partition. The speed had also been greatly accelerated; the journey to Leeds would be performed in about four hours. Blackpool was four or five hours journey, with a few changes of carriages on the way; other distances in proportion. The electric telegraph, adopted in 1838, was not for ten years or more at all generally applied, and it was the duty of Robert to take urgent communications to district officials etc, in the discharge of which he made frequent journeys by rail and other means. He has related curious experiences and 'contretemps' in connection with such owing to irregular services in those days, No great public enterprise recorded in history, either before or since, has spread with anything like equal rapidity to the railway system, nor has any industrial departure benefitted mankind to the same extent as have railways and the introduction of steam power. In 1830 there was absolutely not a metal line in the country; in less than twenty years the country was a complete network of railways, indeed it is wonderful how the work could be done in the time; by the aid of viaducts, bridges, tunnels, embankments and inclines, every obstacle was overcome. These lines were owned by a conglomeration of separate companies. It would be no exaggeration to say that there were ten times as many companies then as there are now, but these, by great spontaneity of action, soon melted themselves into fewer and more powerful concerns by the process of amalgamation, very desirable considering the obstacles they thought proper to put in the way of each others passengers hitherto by inharmonious working. Instead of two companies converging at a junction arranging their trains in such a way that the traveller could pursue his journey with the least possible delay, the trains would be timed to run equi-distant as they could well be arranged, by which means each company expected to take advantage of the other; a most absurd idea as experience has taught us.

Reference has been made to the reaction which affected railway speculators as soon as the bulk of enterprise was launched. They were afraid they had overstepped the need of the times and carried their enthusiasm too far. This revulsion of feeling however, was but momentary; the national faculty of enterprise re-asserted itself; the benefit of railway investment was too apparent; railways continued to multiply and develop, and not withstanding occasional little anxieties on account of depression of trade, have practically never looked back. It was not more than a year after Robert Stockton's appointment at the offices in the Palatine Buildings that the L.&Y. Co. aspired to an improved head quarters, and the splendid stone building on the right side of the incline at the main entrance to the station was built. Comparatively insignificant as it appears to the architecture of to-day, this structure was at the time, a decided ornament to the town and credit to the company of which we are speaking. 'Robert', (the name he commonly bore) of course, removed his quarters along with the rest of the occupants of the 'palatine' to the more spacious apartments called Hunt's Bank. The rooms of the former place were not given up for some time, but continued to be used as supplementary offices to those in the new building.

Directly after the removal Robert was transferred, on his own application, to the Permanent Way department at Miles Platting, but meeting with a slight accident in connection with the loading of some sleepers on a truck, he was on his recovery, retransferred to the Engineer's Office, Hunt's Bank, having been away at Miles Platting about six months. This was in 1847. The duties devolving upon him now became more clearly defined. He attended upon Mr. Hawkshaw, kept the petty cash and several minor books, wrote specifications and quantities, in connection with new work in progress, copied and mounted plans etc. These duties he fulfilled creditably and he continued to win the favour of his superiors. His appearance at this time, that is to say, approaching 30 years of age, was certainly prepossessing. The robustness of his youth has already been remarked upon. He was 5ft 7½ ins high, of broad and well set figure, a healthy complexion and intelligent countenance. There exists several portraits of him about the time named, or a little later, and they quite bear out the above traditions. He had a noble forehead, with dark wavy hair, receding at the temples, but an absence of hairy appendages on the face. Well dressed and circumspect altogether in person, his appearance drew respect and cordiality. The writer has spoken of the educational disadvantage under which his father laboured in his youth. Be it said, to his praise, that by dogmatic perseverance nightly, indeed hourly, consistent with his work, from the time of his arrival in Manchester, he not only acquired the knowledge necessary to his avocation, but in course of a few years had reached the higher educational elements, such as Mathematics, logic etc. He had become a fair grammarian, a ready writer, an presently a tolerable speaker, which latter power served him well in his political experiences. Most conspicuous perhaps among his attainments of knowledge was his repertoire of history. Having a good memory and the historians taste, such was achieved by him with ease, when it would be difficult to most people. But it was a great convenience to those around him to have an encyclopaedia such as he was, for handy reference. His taste in this direction was not of primeval kind, though he was somewhat of an antiquarian, and was very conversant with the Castles and Abbeys of this country. He was also wonderfully familiar with the lineage of our Aristocracy.

His family by this time had increased by the arrival of the first daughter, Mary Jane, who was born at Kent's Place, Ordsall, on 17th of February 1848. A third son, Alfred, was born on 3rd April 1850, but was a delicate child, and only lived until August 20th of the same year. About the year 1849 Robert accompanied Mr. Hawkshaw to Harrogate, to be in attendance on him during the trial which the Company were engaged in at that place. He stayed there some weeks. Several other gentlemen were engaged on the same case, including a Mr. Nolan, Solicitor of Manchester. Mr. Hawkshaw remarked to Robert one day that "he hoped that during the stay he was availing himself of the Harrogate waters". Mr. Nolan rejoined for him "No Sir! But is availing himself of the Harrogate beer". Mr. N. knew as much about Harrogate beer as the object of his remark, seeing that they usually spent their spare time together. Mr. Hawkshaw's (now Sir William) engagement with the L.&Y. Railway became presently that of Consulting Engineer only; his attendance was merely tentative, the Resident Engineer being Mr. Brunlees with Captain Laws assisting. Mr. Cawkwell was General Manager for some years, and was succeeded by Mr. Myles Fenton. These gentlemen, the two last named, may be known to the reader in their subsequent connection, first with the London & North Western and second with the Metropolitan Railway. Mr. Cawkwell was of very humble origin. It is said that he was errand boy at the well known firm of Messrs Agnew, Art Dealers, but from this rose to the General Managership of one of the greatest Railways in the world, viz. The London & North Western, of which Company he is now Vice Chairman. Reference has to be made to Robert's education, and his work and progress. The main object of the writer, however, is to demonstrate the utter conscientiousness and benevolence, the honesty of mind and purpose which animated him towards his fellowmen. No condition of trust, whether put in the way by confidences or the laxity of his superiors, was burden to him. Nor did any object of charity appeal to him in vain. As far as his sphere and his means allowed he was a "good samaritan" personified. His position daily brought him in contact with Chief Officers, Directors, and large shareholders of the Company, who confided in him; and frequently sought his services in the execution of private commissions, both in his own time and in his business capacity. He was an excellent hand at buying and selling and invariably pleased people who acquired such offices of him. Had his field of action been a very limited one, such traits of character as those just described would hardly have been noticeable by reason of their confined operation. But at the head quarters of an important railway in a town like Manchester, the calls upon him, "opportunities", we would prefer to call them, were of no trivial matter. Of course with his increasing family, and his modest income, he was not able to exercise charity to any great extent in a pecuniary way. But his position enabled him to influence more powerful hands when he himself was helpless. He was, moreover, always ready to give a helping hand to anyone in search of a situation, advice or temporary assistance. Dozens of friends and people recommended to him he has aided in this way. He was hospitable; his home was a confluence of friends, many of whom came long distances for the sake of his company. His 'personnel' and conversational powers made him irresistible. His sympathetic sentiment rendered him a centre of support, an arm, as it were, under which all surrounding him found refuge. It was such attribute which made him conspicuous all his life. The writer cannot reflect upon his encouraging voice without feelings of emotion.

Bles't be the man, whose softening heart, Feels all other's pain,
To whom the supplicating eye, Is ever raised in vain,
To him, protection shall be shown, And mercy from above,
Descend on him who thus fulfils, The perfect law of love.

From his infancy he was brought up under the influence of religion. He learnt to read from the Bible; It was his spelling book, so to speak; in fact, at the period of his primary education there were few other books printed. Need it be added he was well versed in that precious volume; that he treasured it, that amongst all his varied literature and the books he collected, this was the fountain head. Hours and hours can the writer remember, in his own childhood, his father pouring over it with great regularity considering his busy life. Any enquiry for information, any instruction wanted upon various points or subjects connected with that book, he was ready to supply, and could easily elucidate. His memory being a powerful one he was himself an index of references and quotations. He was a thorough Christian, the basis of his religion being simply Christ's sermon on the mount, which he was never tired of quoting. His doctrine was of the pure type of Christ's teaching, devoid of all ritualistic complexities. But he studied the writings of all the Evangelists, and had an intelligent conception of them. St. Paul's Epistles, and the work of the Apostle he was much interested in. Nor was he less familiar with the earlier writings, the passage of the Israelites into the promised land, the beautiful story of Joseph and his brethren, Jacob's dream, the trails of Daniel, the prophets, the psalms of David, and other points of the Bible. But his comfort lay in the unmistakeable words of Christ: "Come unto me all ye that are heavy laden, and I will give you rest". "Suffer the little children to come unto me, and forbid them not, for of such is the Kingdom of Heaven". The latter was in keeping with his love of children, whom he was always most tender and careful of. In a scrap book the perusal of which alone affords an insight into his character, there is a print as a frontispiece representing Christ speaking in parables to his disciples, when he says: "Render unto Caesar the things which are Caesar's, and unto God the things that are God's". Matt. XXII, 21.

When residing in Salford, he attended Christ Church, on the Crescent, where the Revd. Hugh Stowell officiated, the Church having been built and endowed by ardent followers of that worthy divine for his purpose. Canon Stowell, an eloquent preacher and an earnest Christian, was so popular that he could, having commended the object to his congregation, at a single collection, command as much as £600 and £700, an amount which, owing to the insipidity of modern congregations, can only be realised nowadays by means of bazaars, the somewhat objectionable method now in vogue at our places of worship. On his removal to Hunt's Bank to reside, some time later, he attended the more convenient Church of St. Anns, which was also administered by a celebrated clergyman, Mr. McGrath. Mr. McGrath was perhaps a little more in accord with Robert's religious feelings than was Canon Stowell. He was more liberal, the Canon being bitter and constant in his attacks upon Roman Catholicism, and anti-royalistic in his opinions. He also made frequent attendances at the Cathedral, or 'Old Church', as it was generally called. Later, however, his religious views seemed to widen, and he espoused the cause of the Wesleyans at their church in Sussex Street, Broughton, and Gravel Lane, Salford. With all its beautiful services, its historic eminences and other attractions, he found fault with the serious anomalies of the Church of England; he found too much stiffness and restraint within its walls, and finally became fully attached to the more homely body of worshippers who followed the example of John Wesley. He was in sympathy with this section of the Church to the end, although his family continued to attend the Cathedral Church and Schools. He had two engravings, one representing the "Escape from Fire", and the other the "death bed of Wesley".

He was thoroughly liberal in his views, especially as he advanced in years, that he admired and extolled the work of all capable religious workers, regardless of sect or creed. Men of eminence in religious creeds of whatever kind, excited his interest. In addition to the names of Stowell, McGrath, were Lee, Spurgeon, Fraser, Moody, and Dr. Talmage, besides as many local men of his time whose names are unknown to the writer. By the kind attention of his daughter-in-law, Sara, at Sale, he was in possession every week with the constant regularity for the last ten years of his life of Dr. Talmage's sermons, published in the Christian Herald. It is a matter of satisfaction that a paper which aims at improving the morals and the religious sentiments of people, as opposed to the mass of crass literature of the opposite kind, should find such widespread circulation as does the paper in question.

To return to his post at the L.&Y. R. Robert continued to strengthen himself in the esteem of his officers. He was, almost about 1850, residing at Fray's Place, Strangeways, already mentioned. Mr. Cawkwell was made Manager, Captain Laws was Robert's superior officer. Meetings were frequently held at Hunt's Bank of the Joint Officials of the London and North Western and Lancashire and Yorkshire Railways, whose interests were common on several portions of the line, and being on friendly terms with one or two gentlemen of the former ompany, he on one occasion expressed his desire to see the Metropolis, whereupon that officer offered to grant him a free pass to travel thither when he was ready to go. The occasion presented itself by the great enterprise of the first International Exhibition of 1851, opened at the Crystal Palace, such a show as the world had not seen before, and which has yet probably never been surpassed. It was contained in a huge building of glass of majestic design, situated in beautiful grounds a few miles from London, where representations of the Art and industry of the entire globe were to be found. However, when the time appointed for the excursion arrived, the passes had been granted, Robert was seen at his post as usual, instead of being 'en route' for London. Being asked the reason for this sudden change of programme, and "why he was not at the Exhibition", he rejoined, "I have got an exhibition at home!" An addition to the family had arrived the preceding night in the person of 'Martha', who was born on the 11th of July 1851, and the projected visit to the South was postponed.

Speaking of exhibitions, the writer once more launches out in the expression of his opinions, and such opinion being in strict analogy to his father's, are an intrinsic part of this work. They are mostly an inheritance from that parent, and others are the outcome of living in an advanced age to that which his father lived. There is a section of narrow minded people who look upon Exhibitions like this of 1851 as a huge mistake from the fact that they teach foreigners who visit them the secrets and inventions which are the groundwork of our commerce. In the writer's opinion, this is all fallacies, the most fallacious. If our commercial success depends on secrecy, our doom is sealed, for it must be evident to all that in these days of inter-communication secrecy is impossible. Besides we must give and take in these matters, and profit if needs be by the numerous exhibitions that are held by our contemporaries abroad. Such exhibitions must be of immense advantage to our rising generations, and to the masses who have no other opportunity of self education than that afforded in this pleasurable way. We, who control one fourth of the human race, must not be behind in displays of this kind, to the vast progeny in different parts of the world. As free trade increases and education grows, and communication becomes easier between one country and another, the writer foresees, at a time not very remote, an age when Europe and other continents will become as one speaking one common language, wars will be a thing of the past, and international exhibitions will have done their quota towards promoting this desirable end.

With the construction of the railways many other improvements and inventions took place. Printing became more general, steam power being applied to its use, books multiplied and became cheaper, envelopes came into use about 1840, postage stamps were introduced in 1839; the sewing machine was invented by Singer, who made the handsome matter of £2,800,000 out of this happy idea; steel pens increased in their use, four million a day being computed to be the consumption of them; steam was rapidly introduced as a means of saving labour in all directions. Its application, however, was not unattended by anxieties. No one today dare say a derogatory word of this valuable modern agent, but when it first came to be introduced it was thought it would do away with the employment of horses, and not only that, but take the labour out of the hands of the artisans and thus their means of earning a livelihood. When steam power was applied to the Lancashire cotton mills there was almost a general uprising of the hands, with stone throwing and rioting. This opposition had to be steadily combated by the capitalists, most of whom could easily foresee that with the large increase which was sure to ensue in manufactures, there would, in other channels be ample employment for men and horses, a prognostication which was fully realised. At the present time, than which the working classes were never better off, it is calculated that the steam engines of the world represent approximately the work of one thousand million men, or more than double the working population of the earth, whose total population amounts to 1,455,923,000 inhabitants. Steam has accordingly trebled man's working power, enabling him to economise his physical strength while attending to his intellectual development.

Lancashire was undoubtedly in the van in all these forward movements; it was the wonderful energy and enterprise of our county which did so much to giving England the lead in the commerce of the world, a most important matter to which our present supreme and unassailable position is largely due. Lancashire has been head foremost in all great movements; we made the first railway; we commenced the agitation and carried the corn laws; we have fed the world, with our cotton, our iron, and our coal; we have made our county capital, "Manchester", familiar all over the world; we can array ourselves with easy modesty with the saying that "What Lancashire says today, England will say tomorrow". As for the Southern Metropolis, we hope you will pardon our egotism, when we say it is, compared to our centre, only a home of fading aristocracy; with its teeming population of foreign refugees, it is sluggish compared to northern industry. Of course, it is compact, and the most populous city in the world, but we, with our score of immense towns within a small radius can influence it in any direction, at will. What care we progressionists about its almost unanimous vote in favour of "constitutionalism", what we call "retrogression"? We are not surprised at their desire to stand still if they cannot recede upon feudalism, for they have always followed in our wake in necessary reforms.

We will now return to Hunt's Bank, not by one of the slow trains of the period but by flash of thought. Very soon after Robert's first appointment under the L.&R. Railway, he amongst his fellow-servants Mr. Joseph Hallam, and Mr. John Croston. These continued to be friends and attachees during all his long service there. Many happy hours have the trio spent together, and many and hot were the political discussions they indulged in, the two holding opposite views to those shared in by their confrere.

Mr. Richard Dyson, and Mr. John Lewis of Oldham Road Station, also Mr. Thorpe, of the Offices at Hunt's Bank, were amongst his associates. The first three gentlemen named are still living well, although in advanced years; are fulfilling indeed similar duties now to those they discharged forty years ago. They are amongst the oldest, (one of them claims to be actually the oldest) servants of the Company.

We heartily wish them a jubilee in their several capacities. Frequent were the excursions they had in company to the seaside and to various places and very enjoyable the outings must have been if one may judge by the stories of their doings. They used their privilege of free railway travelling; Blackpool was often resorted to, and Robert and his friend Thorpe being expert swimmers, they usually indulged in a little exercise of this kind. It was here the acquaintance of Mr. Garlick was formed. Mr. G. was a well known Blackpool character; he was a contractor in the first place in succession to his father, but he afterwards became bathing machine, boat and carriage proprietor, and the keeper in turn of various hotels; the Gynn Inn, near Uncle Tom's Cabin, the Gipsy Tent, South Shore, and other places. Mr. Garlick and Robert grew on very friendly terms, and the former used to join the little parties which went in the way described. Later, he sent his daughter Martha, and his son, Alfred, for a lengthened stay, by which they received lasting benefit. The writer was not able to find out Mr. Garlick on the occasion of his last visit there, and he concludes that the old man has gone to his final resting place. He would like to mention the first visit to the seaside which must have been when he, the writer, was but five or six years old. For it must not be supposed that Robert failed to let his family join in the excursions he indulged in himself. He often took his children, or sections of his large family, along with him. The author of these lines remembers well his first impression of the sea, when he was set down on Talbot Road, just emerging from the Railway Station. What a curious affair that vast expanse of water seemed to him; more like a gigantic field – terminating on the horizon! Closer inspection only added to the strange grandeur and bewilderment. It was a transport to another world. Then came the delightful drive down the breezy promenade to a good dinner at the Wellington Hotel. Then the boats, the donkeys, the bazaars, the buying of presents for absent ones, the day's excitement ending in a sleepy journey home again which seemed never ending.

Prominent in his many qualities was that of punctuality. Many men have looked upon this attribute as a test of general business capacity, demonstrating the ability in other matters with which it appears to have no connection. The writer never knew a better model of punctuality than his father. He went on the principle of being before the appointed time rather than behind it. At work every morning, catching the train, keeping an appointment for business or pleasure he never was late, and seldom in a hurry. He was all his life an early riser. It is no exaggeration to put down the average time of the commencement of his days routine at six thirty a.m.. In the summer time often before six a.m.. He had done half a days work before many people had got the cobwebs out of their eyes, and there is little doubt that by his regularity in this respect his health was materially assisted. He exemplified the saying that "the early bird catches the worm". He used to go off to the market at Shudehill, make advantageous purchases, and come home loaded with vegetables and other articles such as tools etc. then advance a stage in the construction of some articles of furniture, or the repairing of some domestic affairs, long before the majority of his neighbours contemplated turning the blankets off. And we need no inculcation to the fact that such a power coming to him, as it did, without effort, enabled him to anticipate emergencies, imbued with him confidence and saw him at his post at the appointed hour fresh and vigorous. Sunday morning indulgencies were likewise unknown to him. His indulgencies indeed were in 'prompting' bed time. Upto the day when he contracted his last and fatal illness, viz., the 2nd of February 1889, he was up at his accustomed hour, about six a.m.

References

'Railways Then and Now – A World History' *by O S Nock*

The Manchester Guardian, Thursday, 15 February, 1934 - 'Modern Power Station'

'The Life of Sir William Fairbairn, Bart.' *partly by Himself edited and completed by William Pole.*

'Morven – Memory, Myth and Reality' *by Constance M Greiff and Wanda S Gunning.*

'Marketing, Architectural and Engineering Services' *by Weld Coxe (USA)*

CBI News – 25 July 1986 - 'Managing for success'

DTI- Single Market News –September 1991.

'Reinventing the Wheel'– The Construction of British Airways London Eye.

NSC – March 2006 - 'Riding High'.

The Daily Telegraph, 19 December 2015 - 'Politically correct universities "are killing free speech."'

The Daily Telegraph, 8 January 2016 - "Pastor walks free after preaching against 'satanic, hateful Islam.'"

Pictures/Images Credits for Copyright Holders

Cover – Harvesting pre-World War II	© ALAMY Stock Photo
Cover – Churchill	© ALAMY Stock Photo
Cover Battersea Power Station	© Royal Institute of British Architects
Cover – The London Eye	© ALAMY Stock Photo
Cover – Mobile Phone	© Microsoft/Nokia
Cover – Satellite in Space	© ALAMY Stock Photo
1. Harvesting pre-World War II	© ALAMY Stock Photo
3. Evening Chronicle – Britain Now at War	© ALAMY Stock Photo
4. War Declared Official	© ALAMY Stock Photo
5. Evacuee Children World War II	© Imperial War Museum
9. Churchill, "Let us go forward together"	© ALAMY Stock Photo
12. Howtown Ullswater	© Michael Alexander
14. Three Queens at George VI's Funeral	© ALAMY Stock Photo
18. Helga Dances	© Messenger Newspaper Group
20. Rock 'n Roll – The Cellar Style	© Messenger Newspaper Group
23. Thelwall Pipe Bridge	© Ron Horsley, Warrington
27. Ferrybridge 'C' Power Station	© CEGB – Midlands Project Group
28. David and Helga's Small Family Wedding	© Ron Horsley, Warrington
29. David Getting Down to The Works	© CWWood (Bradford) Ltd
30. Tay Bridge Collapse	© ALAMY Stock Photo

33. 12 Foot Diameter Cooling Water Pipe Installation at Didcot Power Station	© Construction Industry Research & Information Association
35. Britannia Bridge Menai Tubular Girder Erection	© Institution of Civil Engineers
37. Battersea Power Station Phase 1	© Royal Institute of British Architects
47. Morven – Princeton NJ	© Morven Museum & Garden, Princeton NJ
52. 'Winter of Discontent'	© ALAMY Stock Photo
59. Pepsi Max 'The Big One'	© ALAMY Stock Photo
60. CBI News – Managing for Success	© CBI
61. J M W Turner's 'Ruskin's View'	© Ashmolean Museum Oxford
66. The London Eye	© ALAMY Stock Photo
69. Self Drive GPS Controlled Combined Harvester	© ALAMY Stock Photo

About the Authors

David Compston CBE

David Compston was born in October 1938. His formative years were spent in remote wartime Cumberland. He was educated at boarding schools in Lincolnshire and then London.

He was one of the last generation of chartered engineers who obtained their academic qualifications by attending 'night school', leading to his career as a consulting engineer with projects across the world.

After retiring, he became involved in Manchester's renaissance including the 2002 Commonwealth Games.

Helga Compston

Helga Compston was born in March 1936. Her time as a wartime evacuee in rural North Yorkshire was the foundation of her formative years. Returning to her family in suburban Manchester, she was educated in the state system.

She was one of the last generation of 'stay at home wives' leading a full family life, while contributing to the work of very many charities and supporting her husband in the promotion of his business.

An avid reader, Helga became a 'student' of history.